What People Are Saying About
The Ten Journeys of Life . . .

"Rabbi Gold has combined the wisdom of a teacher, the knowledge of a scholar, the talent of a storyteller, the experience of a spiritual leader and the insight of a psychologist to create a guide that will help many through the maze of life toward a rich and meaningful path of joy and hope."

Rabbi Dov Peretz Elkins
coauthor, *Chicken Soup for the Jewish Soul*

"Rabbi Gold is a wise and reliable guide on this most important of all journeys."

Rabbi Harold Kushner
author, *When Bad Things Happen to Good People*

"It is not often I can say, 'This book changed my life,' so it is with great enthusiasm that I invite you to read this book. When you write the ethical will that Rabbi Gold speaks about, you will agree it is life-transforming."

Rosita Perez
motivational speaker and president, Creative Living, Inc.

J The Ten Journeys of Life

Walking the Path of Abraham

A Guide to Being Human

MICHAEL GOLD

SiMCHA
PRESS
An Imprint of Health Communications, Inc.®

Deerfield Beach, Florida
www.simchapress.com

Library of Congress Cataloging-in-Publication Data

Gold, Michael, date.
    The ten journeys of life: walking the path of Abraham : a guide
to being human / Michael Gold.
        p.   cm.
    Includes bibliographical references.
    ISBN 1-55874-923-3 (trade paper)
    1. Jewish way of life. 2. Self-actualization (Psychology)—
Religious aspects—Judaism. 3. Life cycle, Human—Religious
aspects—Judaism. 4. Abraham (Biblical patriarch) I. Title.

BM723 .G6 2001
296.7—dc21

                                                    2001024309

Simcha Press, its Logos and Marks are trademarks of Health Communications, Inc.

Publisher: Simcha Press
              An Imprint of Health Communications, Inc.
              3201 S.W. 15th Street
              Deerfield Beach, FL 33442-8190

Cover design by Lisa Camp
Inside book design by Dawn Grove

To Our Children,
Natan, Aliza and Ben,
Your Journeys Are Just Beginning.

CONTENTS

Acknowledgments

The Ten Journeys of Life began as part of my *Rap with the Rabbi* adult education series in my congregation, Temple Beth Torah—Tamarac Jewish Center. We studied the Abraham story and tried to apply its wisdom to the contemporary choices people make. I learned many valuable insights and much wisdom from my students. I have shared these ideas with my congregation in sermons, lectures, counseling and my weekly e-mail spiritual messages, often receiving thoughtful feedback.

As my ideas developed, I taught the same class while serving as scholar-in-residence at the Kislak Adult Center in Lake Como, Pennsylvania, a program run through the New Jersey Young Men's Hebrew Association (YMHA). A week in the Poconos is a marvelous opportunity to clear one's head. It was during that week that I began working on this manuscript. Again, it was my interaction with my students that helped me form some of my greatest insights.

As I explored my own journeys and those of the people I counseled, individuals too numerous to mention helped me with their thoughts and suggestions. I must mention the late Madeline Weil, who was my advisor and confidante. As short as I am tall, we made an odd-looking couple as we sat over lunch swapping ideas. She was taken from us at too young an age, but I am sure her soul is continuing to guide me from the next world.

It was serendipitous that Kim Weiss of Simcha Press sent me an e-mail on an unrelated topic just as I was completing this manuscript and leaving on vacation. She wanted to see it immediately. I spent my week off in California at my computer putting the finishing touches on this work. Both Kim and my editor Susan Tobias had numerous valuable suggestions on making this book more practical and readable. I deeply appreciate their confidence in my work.

Heath Lynn Silberfeld served as my copy editor,

poring over every word and punctuation mark. She challenged me on numerous points and forced me to polish my writing. One day she and I will meet in person and continue our debate on the differences between animals and humans.

As I wrote this book, I constantly reflected on my own journeys through life. I thank God for bringing me Evelyn to be my life partner and fellow traveler. It is not easy to balance the multiple roles of spiritual leader to eight hundred families, writer and lecturer, husband and father. Thank you, Evelyn, for helping me to keep that balance.

I have dedicated this book to my three children Natan, Aliza and Ben. Like most parents, I pray for a way to ensure that their journeys be safe, successful and happy. However, I realize that they must find their own paths. I only hope that, as a parent, I have been a worthy guide and mentor for them.

Introduction

Through you will all the families of the world be blessed.

Genesis 12:3

With ten trials was our father Abraham tried, and he stood steadfast for all of them.

Avot 5:3

A man was lost in the woods. He kept wandering but found himself farther and farther from his home and family. Soon the sun would set, and he was becoming frightened. Would he have to spend the night alone in the woods?

Suddenly the man heard a noise in front of him. It was another man walking toward him through the woods. With a cry, the lost man ran forward, almost knocking over the stranger. "Thank God you have come. Now you can show me the way out of the woods and back to my home."

The other man looked at him. "Sorry. I am also lost. I have no idea how to find our way out of these woods. But now that I have found you, at least we can travel together."

It was the dawn of time. God had created humanity with great hope and anticipation, but most people were evil and corrupt. People did not know the proper path of life. They were lost.

God was obsessed with teaching people the proper path. So God chose one man to become a role model for humanity. The man's name was Abram. God would soon change his name to Abraham, literally "father of nations," in honor of his role as the teacher of humanity.

Abraham was not alone. His whole family became part of God's plan. His relations included three generations. First were Abraham's wife Sarah, then known as Sarai; Sarah's maidservant Hagar, who would become Abraham's second wife; and Abraham's nephew Lot. The second generation included Abraham's older son Ishmael and his younger son Isaac and Isaac's wife Rebecca. The third generation consisted of the two sons of Isaac and Rebecca, Jacob and Essau, and Jacob's wives Rachel and Leah. This family would become humanity's mentors, teaching people the proper path in life.

It all started with Abraham, but first God had to test Abraham to make sure he was worthy of being the pathfinder. In fact, according to an ancient rabbinic tradition, Abraham was given ten different tests. Only by undergoing each of these ten tests was he able to become the leader and teacher God sought. Only through these tests could he bring humanity back onto the proper path.

The ten tests were not examinations like those students take in school. They were not pass/fail tests. They were more like trials or ordeals that Abraham had to endure and complete. In fact, each was a learning experience. Perhaps the best way to describe these ten tests is as ten journeys. Abraham had to go through the ten journeys of life. By successfully completing each of them, Abraham became the mentor for all humanity.

Each of us must travel these same ten journeys as we go through our lives. Each of us is tested ten times, going through ten trials and ordeals; each of us becomes more human as we travel the ten journeys of life.

This book is a guide to being human. As humans, we share something with the animal kingdom. We live a material existence; we eat, drink, sleep, have sexual relations, reproduce our species, get sick and eventually we die. However, as humans we are also profoundly different from the animal kingdom. As the psalmist taught regarding humans, "Thou has made him but little lower than the angels, and have crowned him with glory and honor" (Psalms 8:6). We carry within us the breath of God. (The Hebrew word for soul, *neshama*, literally means "breath.") A major theme of these ten journeys is how we can rise above our animal nature and find the breath of God that echoes within each of us.

Rabbi Alvin Fine once said, "Birth is a beginning, and death is a destination, and life is a journey." Life is actually ten different journeys. We all travel most of them; many of us travel them all. We may travel them in a different order than Abraham did, and different journeys may become crucial at different times in our lives. We may successfully complete one of these journeys, only to discover later that we must begin that particular journey again. However, travel we must if we are to live successful lives.

As we travel the ten journeys of life, Abraham and his family become our mentors. In this book, I begin with their story, their mistakes and their search for their proper path. I tell the stories of Abraham and his family, as they appear in the Torah (the Five Books of Moses, which form the beginning of what Jews call the Hebrew scripture, or Tanach, and Christians call the Old Testament).

In telling the story of Abraham, I also share the midrash, the many rabbinic stories and interpretations that elaborate upon and provide insights into the biblical text. These biblical stories and rabbinic legends are only our jumping-off point. This is a book about how to live today. It is filled with practical wisdom. This is a book on how to be fully human, living by God's light.

Each chapter contains a section near the end called "Guideposts for Your Journey." Each is addressed to you, as if you have come into my office for counseling and advice. In fact, Guideposts for Your Journey grew out of hundreds of counseling sessions with my synagogue members and outsiders, both Jews and Christians. This section is filled with practical wisdom for those searching for the path. I wrote it with the hope that this book will be more than theoretical and will provide real hands-on coaching for becoming more fully human.

Sometimes we humans feel lost. However, we are never alone. Together, we will find the proper path. Looking at Abraham and his family as our guide, let us begin the journey together.

Because we humans can never fully know God, we assume as we begin that God is with us. Even Moses, God's greatest prophet, could not know God face to face. He could only see God's back (Exodus 33:23). He could not see what God is, only what God does. Even Moses had only an incomplete picture—a metaphor.

For each of these journeys, we relate to God

differently and use different metaphors to describe our relationship with God. As we travel, though, we need never feel lost or alone. God is always with us. For each of the ten journeys,

God is our Guidepost.

1

Identity

The Journey from Childhood to Adulthood

The Lord said to Abram, "Go forth from your land, your birthplace, your father's house, to the land that I will show you."

Genesis 12:1

Man stamps many coins with one die and they are all alike one to another, but the King of Kings, the Holy One, stamps all humans with the die of the first person, and no one is like any other one.

Sanhedrin 4:5

When Rabbi Zusya was about to die, his students gathered around him. They saw Rabbi Zusya's eyes break out into tears. "Our master," they said with deep concern, "why are you crying? You have lived a good, pious life, and left many students and disciples. Soon you are going on to the next world. Why cry?"

Rabbi Zusya responded, "I see what will happen when I enter the next world. Nobody will ask me, why was I not Moses? I am not expected to be Moses. Nobody will ask me why was I not Rabbi Akiba? I am not expected to be Rabbi Akiba. They will ask me why was I not Zusya? That is why I am crying. I am asking, why was I not Zusya?"

It all begins with leaving home.

The first journey each of us must make is to leave home. We must move from childhood to adulthood. We must separate from our parents and seek our own identities. We must begin the process of discovering who are we and why God put us on this earth.

God wanted to make a covenant with Abraham. First God told him to leave home. God said to Abram (his original name), "Go forth from your land, your birthplace, the house of your father, to a land that I will show you." Abraham could not begin his sacred task until he separated from his parents and left behind his childhood.

We first notice the language, the three places Abraham must leave—his land, his birthplace, the house of his father. The rabbis have noted that it is easiest to leave *our land*; this represents the physical act of moving out. Many of us leave at around age eighteen, when we go off to college, join the military or get married. Physical leaving may involve simply loading a car with our belongings and going off to a school dormitory. We may feel independent, but we are far from being adults.

It is harder to leave *our birthplace*; this represents economic independence. We must find a way to support ourselves and not be dependent upon our parents for our physical needs. Some of us gain this in our early or midtwenties, some later and some never achieve it. It is not our parents' responsibility to support us forever.

It is hardest to leave *the house of our father*; this represents psychologically asserting our own identity. What differentiates us from our parents, and how can we be our own selves? People who grow up in very controlling homes may never achieve that psychological independence.

Through the teenage years and well into our twenties, each of us must leave in these three different ways. We must physically move out of our parents' home. We must stop being economically dependent upon our parents. We must psychologically forge our own identity independent of our parents. These are three transitions—each more difficult than the last. Like Abraham, each of us has three different leavings.

Certainly we must leave our parents' home. But where are we going to? The Hebrew text provides a powerful hint of the answer. The exact words are *lech lecha*, which is translated as "go forth." The precise translation is "go to yourself." Our primary task as young adults is to leave our parents and *go to ourselves.*

There is a very famous midrash (rabbinic legend) that teaches about Abraham's father Terach owning an idol store. One day Abraham broke all the idols except the largest one. When his father saw the merchandise ruined, he cried out, "What happened?" Abraham replied, "The big one became angry and broke all the others." "That is impossible! They are only wood and

stone." "So why do you sell them as gods?" answered
Abraham (Genesis Rabbah 38:13).

This was the beginning of young Abraham leaving
home and forging his own identity. Surely Terach
dreamed that some day his son would inherit his idol business and keep it in the family, but Abraham would have
none of his father's idolatrous business. He had begun the
process of *going to himself,* forging his own identity.

Another midrash is about Abraham's journey from
home. When he was in his father's house, Abraham
resembled a vial of precious myrrh closed with a tight-
fitting lid. As long as he stayed within his parents' home,
nobody could smell the fragrance. However, once he
began his journey, the lid was opened and fragrance was
disseminated (Genesis Rabbah 34:2). So all of us, in
order to make ourselves felt in the world, need to begin
the process of leaving home.

From Childhood to Adulthood

A famous passage in the Talmud teaches, "There are
three partners in the creation of a human being—

father, mother and God" (Niddah 31a). Our father and mother gave us our unique genetic code, the biological source of our physical attributes and predispositions. God gave us our unique soul, charging it to accomplish its unique mission upon this earth. Our journey begins when our soul enters our body and we start living our embodied existence here on earth.

When God created the first man, He taught, "Therefore a man shall leave his mother and father and cleave unto his wife" (Genesis 2:24). As I tell every young bride and groom who sit with me to plan their wedding, "First you must *leave* before you can *cleave*."

Our first journey takes us from childhood to adulthood. It begins when we realize that we are not part of our parents but a separate entity. It continues as we are weaned off our mother's milk, as we take our first wobbly steps away from our parents, as we go off to school or summer camp, as we begin to discover our own talents and unique destiny.

The work of this journey becomes more intense during the teen years. Now we must assert our own identity, which often means rebelling against our parents' values and the rules of our home. We are constantly testing the limits. We are guided by peers rather than parents. If we seek adult guidance, we often prefer to turn to other mentors—a coach, a teacher, a school counselor, a youth leader, a clergy person. The journey from our parents is a difficult one in these years, often compared to a whitewater rafting trip down churning rapids. We will get wet, we will feel both frightened and thrilled, but in the end most of us will come through safely.

As the teen years end, we finally are ready to move out on our own. Moving out does not happen all at once. We move out physically but find ourselves coming home when crises hit. We eventually achieve some financial independence. Then comes the hardest move of all: separating from our parents and asserting our own identity. Being on our own, we finally discover who we really are.

If parents are wise, they will guide us on this journey. They will give us roots and values but will not seek to control us or claim ownership of us. As the poet Kahlil Gibran beautifully taught in his work *The Prophet:*

Your children are not your children. They are the sons and daughters of Life's longing for itself. They

*came through you but not from you, and though
they are with you they belong not to you.*

*You may give them your love but not your
thoughts, for they have their own thoughts. You may
house their bodies but not their souls, for their souls
dwell in the house of tomorrow, which you cannot
visit, not even in your dreams. You may strive to be
like them, but seek not to make them like you. For
life goes not backward nor tarries with yesterday*
(Gibran, 1993).

Honoring Parents

Even as children leave their homes, they must honor
the parents who raised and guided them. This law is so
fundamental to human civilization that it is one of the
Ten Commandments: "Honor your father and mother"
(Exodus 20:12). Honoring parents provides the link
between generations.

What does honor mean? It does not mean to love our
parents. Family is too important to be subject to the
vagaries of love. Nor does it mean to obey our parents.

Certainly honor means to listen carefully and consider the advice of those who raised us. However, after dutifully respecting their advice and counsel, leaving home is about making our own decisions.

In rabbinic tradition, there are two aspects of honoring parents. One is to respect and value the dignity of their position. One must do nothing to detract from their standing as mother or father. The ruling, which uses masculine language, teaches that a son should not stand in his father's place, nor sit in his place, nor contradict him, nor tip the scales in an argument against him.

The second aspect of honor is providing for one's parents when they become needy, particularly in old age. The ruling states that the son "must supply his father with food and drink, provide him with clothes and footwear, and assist his coming in and going out of the house" (Kiddushin 31b).

As children enter the adult years, there is a natural tension between parents and children. On one hand, children must leave home and seek their own identity. On the other hand, children must then turn around and honor the parents who raised them. The prophet Malachi recognized this tension. He spoke of the messianic age when God will "turn the hearts of the sons toward the fathers, and the hearts of the fathers toward the sons" (Malachi 3:24). When the Messiah comes, parents and children will get along. In our unredeemed age, there is always a natural tension.

This natural tension can be particularly exacerbated by parents who are controlling and manipulative or who refuse to let go of their children. It can also be exacerbated by selfish, unappreciative children who refuse to recognize their parents' devotion and sacrifice. In the ideal world, parents guide their children to find their own niches and identities, and children appreciate and honor those parents, caring for them in their old age. In this ideal world, parents raise their children to have both roots and wings.

Go to Yourself

In the classic Hasidic story retold at the beginning of this chapter, Rabbi Zusya's greatest fear was not that he was never Moses, never Akiba. It was that in the next world he would be asked, "Why were you not Zusya?" He feared God would ask him, "Why did you not fulfill your unique destiny, which is the reason I put you on the earth?" This simple story reflects perhaps the most powerful teaching of our shared biblical traditions: Our soul has a unique destiny. We are not on this earth by random chance but have been put here to fulfill a divine purpose.

Each of us has a mission and a calling. In a beautiful statement about the uniqueness of each and every human being, the rabbis teach, "Man stamps many coins with one die and they are all alike one to another, but the King of Kings, the Holy One, stamps all humans with the die of the first person, and no one is like any other one" (Sanhedrin 4:5). No two humans have precisely the same calling on this earth. Even identical twins, although they share genetic information, have a separate set of life experiences that contribute to their uniqueness. Every human being is totally irreplaceable, for no two people are born into the exact same circumstances. No one else can do what another was put on this earth to do.

Our first great journey of life, leaving home, also leads us to find our particular calling. Some of us know immediately, from the earliest days of childhood, why

God put us on this earth. Some of us spend much of our lives searching. Some of us find our calling as young adults, some in the middle years, some only upon retirement from the work force. Some never quite find it. Our very language reflects this sense that each of us has a unique mission: We often speak of young people who are still "finding themselves."

For some, the calling comes in a moment of revelation. Moses was a shepherd, happily married, settled and working for his father-in-law. Suddenly he came upon a bush that burned but was not consumed. A voice cried out from the bush telling Moses, "Go before Pharaoh and tell him, 'Let my people go'" (Exodus 8:1). Moses tried every excuse to avoid his calling. In the end, it was his destiny and he had to go. As the prophet Amos teaches, "My Lord God has spoken, who cannot prophecy" (Amos 3:8).

How do we know our true calling? Rick Jarow, in his beautiful set of audiotapes entitled *Your Life's Work*, explains:

> *The sense of calling has its origins in the deepest*
> *recesses of our being. It is the call of the heart, which*

is not necessarily heard as a physical voice, but often
as a feeling, as a yearning, or even as a restless sense
that something is missing in our life. This sense of
calling is literally the breath of the divine emerging
through the clamor and haste of the world. To follow
it is to make your very life beautiful no matter what
the circumstances; to listen to it is to respect yourself;
to honor it is the first step in the creation of an open,
free and compassionate society; and to cultivate it is
the work that pleases the inner being. And when the
inner being is pleased, the world will smile upon it
(Jarow, 1998).

When varied human beings come together, each following a unique calling, they create a beautiful, complex
masterpiece. Each has a role in perfecting the world as a
kingdom of God. A story about Sir Michael Conti
rehearsing the London Symphony to play Beethoven's
Ninth Symphony illustrates this truth. The full orchestra
and a large chorus were singing the fourth movement
when the piccolo player suddenly stopped playing. He
said to himself, "Everybody else is so loud, they cannot
hear me anyhow. What is the difference if I play?" Sir

Conti suddenly stopped the rehearsal and shouted, "Where is the piccolo?! I do not hear the piccolo!"

In the Recesses of Our Soul

In order to explore more deeply the meaning of the search for our mission, I share one more classic Jewish story.

A man named Isaac lived in a little house in a small town way out in the country. Isaac had a wife and children, and he worked hard to provide for them. There never seemed to be enough money to meet his family's needs.

One night Isaac had a strange dream: If he traveled to a distant city and found a famous bridge in the center of the city, he would find a buried treasure. When he woke up, he wondered about the dream but soon dismissed it as he went about his work. The next night he had the same dream again, and again for several more nights. Finally, he knew what he had to do. He had to travel to the distant city and search for the treasure.

In those days travel was not easy. The journey to the distant city would take many days and be filled with perils. Isaac had never traveled far from home before. He kissed his wife and children goodbye and left on the long journey. After many days and many adventures, he arrived in the big city.

Isaac was overwhelmed by the sights and sounds of city life. Never had he seen so many people in one place before. He found the bridge in the center of the city and began to dig under it. Though he dug a number of holes, he could not find the treasure. Soon a police officer approached and asked, "What are you doing?"

Isaac was frightened. "Please, Officer, I can explain. I had a dream that if I traveled to this distant city and dug under the bridge, I would find a treasure. I have been digging, but so far I have found nothing."

The police officer stared at Isaac, as if debating whether to arrest him. "This is very strange. I also had a dream. In my dream, it shows a small home far away in the country belonging to someone named Isaac. In my dream, if I dig under Isaac's fireplace, there will be a treasure." Isaac was

*dumbfounded. How did the officer know his name
and of his little house in the country?*

*Isaac traveled home as quickly as possible and
immediately started digging under the fireplace.
There he found a great treasure that provided for
him and his family the rest of his days.*

That is the irony of our life's search for a mission. The
journey begins when we leave home. Yet ultimately we
must return home, go deep within ourselves, and
explore our gifts, our dreams, our passions, our mentors
and our deepest desires to know why God chose to put
us on this earth.

Guideposts for Your First Journey: From Childhood to Adulthood

1. This journey begins with a self-evaluation of your
   relationship with your parents. Have you truly left
   home? Are you living your life independent of your
   parents? Do you have your own place to live? Are
   you economically self-sufficient? Have you
   achieved some psychological independence? Are
   you able to make personal decisions without

having your parents affirm them? Have you established your own identity?

2. Finding independence must be balanced with honoring one's parents. The first step in honoring parents is respecting their dignity and position. Do you visit them on holidays or invite them to share holiday meals with you? Do you examine family pictures and discuss family history with them? Do you phone them to keep in touch? Do you spend regularly scheduled time with them, either in person or by phone? If you live out of town, do you visit on a regular basis according to your budget? Have you made provisions for their care in their old age? If your parents are deceased, do you visit them at the cemetery or say appropriate memorial prayers?

3. One of life's most difficult tasks is finding the balance between asserting independence from our parents and honoring them. Honoring does not mean obeying. It does mean listening and respecting experience and wisdom. If your relationship with your parents is out of balance, professional counseling may be appropriate.

4. Even as you honor your parents, you must seek

your unique mission in life. Take out a pen and paper and begin a careful self-evaluation, or keep a journal, asking the following questions: What unique gifts do you have? Are you good with people? Are you artistic? Do you love solving problems? Are you a writer? Do you have a taste for adventure? Do you have unusual athletic talent? Can you play a musical instrument? Do you enjoy solving people's problems?

The Bible describes Bezalel as an artisan charged with creating the portable tabernacle the Israelites carried through the desert. It describes him as having "the wisdom of God" (Exodus 35:31). Each of us has been given unique gifts by God. Your life's mission begins with discovering your particular special gifts and developing those talents. Consider this wise saying: "What I am is God's gift to me. What I do is my gift to God."

5. Explore what are you passionate about. What do you dream about late at night when you are unable to sleep? If you had only one year to live, what would you accomplish with your life? What do you want to be remembered for? In what areas are you absolutely

irreplaceable? If you had enough money to meet your financial needs, how would you use your time?

6. Who are your mentors? Who are the teachers that attract you? For many people, their parents are their mentors. Still, the relationship with parents is always complex; part of your job is to break away from them and establish your own identity. Who are the other major individuals, both living and dead, both those you know personally and those you know only by reputation, you admire? Who can serve as your role models and guides? Who do you want to be proud of your work?

7. Sometimes we find we have been pursuing one goal only to find with hindsight that our life's work was altogether something else. For example, in the powerful movie *Mr. Holland's Opus,* Richard Dreyfuss portrays a high-school music teacher who dreams of being a composer. He is frustrated by his lack of progress in pursuing his dream. Only when he is about to retire and his students pay tribute to his years of work does he realize what his true mission in life has been: touching the hearts of his students with his love of music. Looking back on

your life so far, is there a mission you have been working to fulfill?

8. Sometimes you need to take time out of your life to consider your mission. You need to disappear from work and family obligations for a brief period. Even a week in the mountains or a day at the beach can help.

   During one particularly difficult year, the demands of my synagogue were pulling me in too many directions. I had lost my focus. I took a week by myself in the Pocono Mountains to think and reevaluate. My strength as a teacher has always been applying the wisdom of the past to the human realities of today. I needed to concentrate on this mission. That summer is when I began writing this book.

   Each of us ought to study our own lives at times, perhaps coming away with some deep and useful insight: "Aha! This is why God put me on this earth."

9. Try to write your life's mission as an "elevator speech." Suppose you were on an elevator moving down from the fifth floor with a total stranger. You have about thirty seconds, until you reach the first floor, to describe your life's mission. What would you say?

Three Parents

We are here on this earth because of the partnership of *three* parents: our mother, our father and God. Our mother and father give us our physical being. God gives us our spiritual being, our unique identity and unique purpose. We must honor our parents, who raised and nurtured us. Ultimately, we honor God when we fulfill His life plan for us.

This is a profound theological message, one that I have used frequently in my own rabbinical counseling. When people are sad or lost, depressed or troubled, I often ask, "Why did God place you on this earth?" As we search for an answer, healing begins.

We human beings are not on this earth by random chance. We are not here as a result of blind forces of evolution or arbitrary chemical processes. We do not live by the luck of some blind, cosmic forces. On the contrary, we are who we are precisely because God desired for us to be this way.

The prophet Jeremiah taught, "Before I created you in the womb, I selected you. Before you were born, I consecrated you" (Jeremiah 1:5). Each of us is part of this divine plan. We have infinite value. We are absolutely precious in God's eyes. We are created in God's image, because God desired us to be on this earth at this time, in this place, with these particular skills and talents.

We are not the same as our parents. They certainly raised us and gave us our values, and therefore they are worthy of honor, but we are not here to live their lives or fulfill their dreams. We have our own unique gifts to give the world and our own mission to complete. That mission comes from the Creator.

As we search for our unique mission in this world, we must always remember that

God is our Parent.

Maturity

The Journey from
Self-Indulgence to Self-Control

There was a famine in the land, and Abram went down to Egypt to sojourn there, for the famine was severe in the land.

Genesis 12:10

The good inclination attaches itself only from the age of thirteen and onward. . . . The evil inclination attaches itself from youth to old age.

Ecclesiastes Rabbah 4:13

A certain man lived a mediocre life, neither very good nor very bad. When his time came to die, he did not know whether he would end up in heaven or in hell.

He made it to the next world and was taken to a lovely home. A servant entered and told him he was to live there by himself. If he wanted anything, all he had to do was ring the bell and the servant would come.

The man made himself comfortable. He rang the bell for his favorite food to eat, and the servant brought it to him. He rang the bell for a game for entertainment, and it was brought to him. He even requested a young woman to meet his physical needs. She came, did her job and left immediately. Every one of his needs and desires was taken care of, but still he remained alone.

The man found himself becoming more and more lonely. His appetites were all satisfied, but the man realized that there must be something more. Finally, when he could stand it no more, he rang the bell and told the servant, "I have had enough of heaven. I am lonely. I think I would like to see what hell is like."

*The servant answered, "Where do you think you
are?"*

Animals live by their appetites. Part of what makes us
human is the realization that we cannot have whatever
our appetites' desire. We must learn to delay gratification, control our appetites and live with a greater purpose in mind. It is a difficult lesson for every young
person to learn, but controlling one's appetites is the
road to maturity.

God had promised Abraham the entire land of
Canaan. Abraham had left his home in Haran and
traveled a long distance to finally set foot in the
Promised Land. When he arrived, he explored the
entire land, building altars and viewing the landscape.
Abraham felt at home and was ready to live by God's
promise in his own land.

However, God had other plans for Abraham. God
brought a famine to the land, causing Abraham to leave
and flee to Egypt. His desire to live in the Promised
Land would have to wait.

Perhaps God was simply testing Abraham's faith.
Trust in God was a keystone to the future covenant God

would make with Abraham. Nonetheless, Abraham had to learn another lesson, the same one that every child must learn from his or her parents: Immediate gratification is not the path to maturity, and everything valuable in life is worth the wait. Abraham would not immediately possess the land. It would happen only after a long wait.

The Path to Maturity

Perhaps the most important part of the journey from childhood to adulthood is learning self-control and self-discipline so we can conquer our appetites for immediate gratification and discipline our lives for a greater purpose. In exploring this idea, we begin with one of the most profound rabbinic teachings in all of Jewish tradition, one that goes to the heart of what makes humans different from mere animals.

The Torah uses the Hebrew word *yitzer* ("formed") in reference to the creation of both humans and animals: "The Lord God formed (*yitzer*) the man of the dust of the ground, and breathed into his nostrils the breath of life, and man became a living soul" (Genesis 2:7). "The Lord God formed (*yitzer*) out of the ground every beast of the field, and every fowl of the air" (Genesis 2:19). However, *yitzer* is spelled differently in these two instances, with the Hebrew letter *yud* used once for the creation of animals and twice for the creation of humans. In this one tiny letter is the key to the Torah's message about humanity.

The term *yetzer*, from the same root as *yitzer*, has a double meaning in Hebrew. It means "formed" and "inner drive." Both animals and humans have a *yetzer* that underlies and defines their behavior. The rabbis note that the slight difference in spelling is because animals have only one *yetzer* while humans beings have two (Berachot 61a).

Animals behave basically by instinct. They follow patterns of behavior that have been hardwired into their brains from birth. Certainly animals are capable of some learning, but they do not make moral choices. When a coyote attacks a farmer's sheep, he is simply doing what coyotes are hardwired to do. One would not say that such a coyote is doing wrong. Whether it is a salmon swimming upstream to its spawning ground, a dog in heat copulating with another dog or a lion attacking its prey, animals are following instinct. Even the ox in Exodus that gores continually is simply following inbred behavior, and the ox's owner is liable for damages. One would not call the ox a sinner. As I often say in my sermons, "Horses don't need Yom Kippur." Animals have a single inner drive, a single inclination, what the rabbis call a single *yetzer*.

We humans are fundamentally different from animals. We are born with a minimum number of instinctual behaviors, such as sucking and crying, which help us survive our youngest years. Mostly we are blank slates ready to be molded (Avot 4:25). According to one brilliant rabbinic insight, we humans have two *yetzers*, two inner drives or inclinations, which struggle with one another. These two inner drives define our behavior throughout our lives. The rabbis call these the *yetzer hara*, the evil inclination, and the *yetzer hatov*, the good inclination.

The *yetzer hara* consists of those primitive drives within us that seek immediate gratification. Some would relate them to what Sigmund Freud called the id. The *yetzer hara* is the sexual drive, the drive for violence, the drive for acquisition, the emotion of anger, self-aggrandizement, all out of control. The evil inclination is that part of each one of us that says, "I want what I want and I want it now!" These drives are our primitive appetites, necessary for survival but in desperate need of control.

The *yetzer hatov* is the drive to be altruistic. It is the part of us willing to delay gratification, practice self-control, share with others, sacrifice for a greater good and do the right thing. Some would relate it to Freud's superego.

For humans, life is a constant struggle between these two inclinations, between "I want what I want and I want it now" and "Do the right thing." We see this when we decide whether or not to indulge in a forbidden sexual encounter, whether to spend or save money, whether to act out our anger, even whether or not to eat ice cream when we are dieting.

Still, we need our *yetzer hara*. Without it, according to rabbinic tradition, no one would build a house or marry. According to a famous legend, the rabbis once captured the *yetzer hara* and hid it in a barrel (Yoma 69a). For three days nothing happened, no one went to work, even the chickens stopped laying eggs. The rabbis had to let the *yetzer hara* go.

This passage teaches that we need our primitive appetites. We need our appetite for food and drink for physical survival. But that hunger out of control leads to gluttony and unhealthy behavior. We need our sexual drive if we are ever to choose a spouse and create a family. But sexuality out of control leads to promiscuity, disease and the breakdown of families. We need our appetite for material items if we are to work to provide for ourselves and our families. But our appetite for acquisition out of control leads to greed and sometimes to criminal behavior. We need our appetite for anger if we are to stand up to evil and injustice. But anger out of control leads to violence and hatred. We need a certain amount of selfishness if we are to survive in a threatening world. But total self-aggrandizement prevents us from ever moving beyond our needs and serving those around us.

The key is not to destroy the *yetzer hara* but to control it and sublimate it for good. Ben Zoma taught, "Who is strong? Whoever controls their evil inclination" (Avot 4:1). Self-control and the delay of gratification are the beginning of maturity.

What Adulthood Means

Children are born neither good nor evil, but rather like blank slates. Every human struggles internally between good and evil, between good and evil inclinations. And when the Bible says that humans are created in the image of God, it means that humans, like God, are able to make moral choices.

The rabbis offer another profound insight about this struggle between our two *yetzers*. The *yetzer hara*, the evil inclination, is present in full force from the moment of birth. We are born with our appetites intact, crying out to be satisfied. After Noah and the flood, God realized that "the devisings of man's mind are evil *from his youth*" (Genesis 8:21). Babies cry until their physical needs are met, and they do not care who they disturb. Children seek immediate gratification and can be selfish and sometimes cruel. Anyone who claims that children are naturally good, that society corrupts them, has never spent time caring for children. Children certainly have the potential to do good, but their natural inclination is toward selfishness and immediate gratification. They must be taught to do good.

The *yetzer hatov,* or good inclination, is only present in potential at birth. It needs to be carefully nurtured and developed, and it only enters in full force at the moment of adulthood (Ecclesiastes Rabbah 4:13). (According to rabbinic law, adulthood begins at thirteen for boys, twelve for girls. That is why a father says at his son's bar mitzvah, "Blessed is He Who freed me from responsibility for his sins." As I raise my teenagers, I would say the *yetzer hatov* is not there in full force until at least eighteen, if not later.)

This insight points to the essence of parenting. *Parents must carefully nurture their children in the art of self-control.* Children must learn that they cannot have what they want immediately when they want it. Children must manage their appetites for food, for money, for material possessions, and once they become teens they must manage their appetites for sexual satisfaction and other forms of immediate gratification. They must learn to move beyond themselves and think about how their actions affect those around them.

Without proper parenting, children never develop the self-control necessary for maturity. Perhaps the most famous example from classical literature is found in the novel *Lord of the Flies* by William Golding. A group of youngsters is shipwrecked on an island. Within a short time, the worst of their instincts take over, and their society spirals downward to cruelty and violence.

The good inclination needs to be nurtured and developed, and the evil inclination must be brought under control. Maturity begins when we realize that we cannot immediately have whatever our appetites desire.

The Ego and Free Will

Using Freud's terminology, I identify the *yetzer hara* or evil inclination with the id, the primitive appetites that need to be controlled and sublimated. I identify the *yetzer hatov* or good inclination with the superego, the conscience that is imparted to us by our parents or society and that teaches us self-control, altruism and delayed gratification.

Freud also spoke of the ego, that part of us able to consciously make decisions. We humans have the ability to choose. We also must take responsibility for those choices. Free will is God's greatest gift to us. It is the part of us that makes us most godlike and the essence of the teaching that "we were created in the image of God" (Genesis 1:27).

Remember some of the cartoons you watched as a child? A character frequently had to make a moral choice. On one shoulder stood a little devil, urging him or her in one direction. On the other shoulder stood a little angel, urging the opposite choice. It is a childish description of the profound struggle between our good and evil inclinations in each of us.

Our lives are filled with decisions. In fact, motivational speaker Anthony Robbins has built a very successful career lecturing that our lives are composed of the decisions we make day in and day out. Maturity is the ability to make the right decision, the one that will lead to the greater good. This often means delaying immediate gratification while maintaining a vision of that greater good. It means decisions based on our own community's long-term interest, even if our appetites are screaming for us to do otherwise.

Unfortunately, in contemporary America we too often tend to pursue immediate gratification. Author and radio personality Dennis Prager has commented that we mistake fun for happiness, and we search for immediate pleasure rather than the long-term achievement that will ultimately bring us happiness. In fact, in *Happiness Is a Serious Problem,* Prager teaches that fun and happiness are really opposites: "To understand why fun doesn't create happiness and can even conflict with it, we must understand the major difference between fun and happiness: *Fun is temporary; happiness is ongoing.* Or to put it another way, fun is during, happiness is during and after" (Prager, 1998, p. 47). He provides an illustration of an amusement park. Going to an amusement park might be fun, it's a diversion, it's relaxing, but after leaving the park, one's happiness has not increased one iota. A lifetime of amusement parks is not a lifetime of happiness. So what is the key to happiness? Prager continues:

> *Everything that leads to happiness involves pain. While it is widely acknowledged that success in professional life and in sports, to cite two examples, is associated with pain (e.g., hard work, self-discipline, delayed gratification), success in happiness is almost never associated with pain.*
>
> *As a result, many people avoid some of the very*

things that would bring them the deepest happiness, such as marriage, children, intellectually challenging pursuits, religious commitment, and volunteer work. . . . As the Psalmist put it millennia ago, "Those who sow in tears will reap in joy (Psalms 126:5)" (Ibid., p. 53).

Happiness does not come through fun; on the contrary, it comes through pain, sacrifice, commitment, sweat. Achieving happiness is not relaxing; on the contrary, it is hard work. In the Bible, Abraham had to learn that real achievement comes through delayed gratification. It would take him years to settle in the Promised Land.

Dennis Prager's thesis grows out of Jewish tradition. Pirkei Avot, the beautiful tractate of Talmud that contains the ethical maxims of the great rabbis, teaches the key to happiness. "Ben Hey Hey said, 'In accordance with the pain is the reward'" (Avot 5:27). The reward of happiness comes only with great effort. Maturity is the ability to delay gratification and put in the real effort that ultimately leads to success and happiness.

Effort and Reward

Throughout the following chapters, I present the many rewarding journeys of life. I speak about building families, achieving prosperity, caring for our physical bodies, handling pain, finding spirituality, improving the community, as well as recovery when we find ourselves on the wrong path. These efforts begin with maturity and require difficult and often painful decisions. All involve huge efforts and delayed gratification.

Examples abound. Michael Jordan may be the world's greatest basketball player, but he did not achieve this stature overnight. He practiced his shots, his plays, day in and day out, year after year. It took time, effort, pain. Michelle Kwan is one of the world's greatest figure skaters because she arose before dawn year after year to practice for hours every day. The great artists, musicians, scientists, novelists, teachers and scholars all put hours of sweat and toil into their successes. Unfortunately, today we want everything instantaneously.

As a rabbi, I see people who want instant spirituality. They want some magic to connect them with God. I recall a woman who called me after Yom Kippur. She had come to holiday services after not having set foot in a synagogue for many years. She sat for a half hour and then left. She later called me and complained, "Rabbi, I waited a half hour for something to happen spiritually, but nothing happened. So I left. Maybe I'll try the Kabbalah Center."

Jewish spirituality, like all spiritual traditions, is a long, slow process. It begins with learning to read Hebrew and finding a home in the prayer book. It includes the disciplines of prayer, of study, of *mitzvot*. It is deeply rewarding but takes time and effort. I say more about this in chapter seven.

Some people want instant professional success. They do not want to work their way up or pay their dues, but rather to start at the top. They want to be made a partner the first day on the job.

Success in life is never instantaneous. It takes time, effort, sacrifice. Perhaps it is worthwhile to share the description of one man's career:

1832   Lost job, defeated for state legislature.

1833   Failed in business.

1835   Sweetheart died.

1836   Had nervous breakdown.

1838   Defeated for Speaker of the House of
        Representatives.

1843   Defeated for nomination to Congress.

1848   Lost renomination.

1849   Rejected for land officer.

1854   Defeated for U.S. Senate.

1856   Defeated for nomination as vice president.

1858   Again defeated for U.S. Senate.

1860   Elected president.

Of course I am speaking of Abraham Lincoln. Success came only with years of persistence.

Some people want instant relationships. They believe they can fall in love in a moment and that love will carry them through fifty years of marriage. As Oscar Hammerstein wrote in the musical *South Pacific*, they expect that some enchanted evening they will see a stranger, that love will be instantaneous. All they have to do is fly to the stranger's side and make him or her their own. Unfortunately, all too often, a few years later the old relationship has worn away a little, the excitement is gone. We look for something newer, flashier, more exciting. Another stranger appears across another crowded room. We turn in the old flame for a newer model. Life becomes a series of short-term relationships.

In truth, every relationship needs time, energy, nurturing. A marriage does not last fifty years without hard work to make it successful. Instant infatuation, instant attraction, instant chemistry and instant lust are not instant love.

The same is true for raising children: Instant parenthood does not exist, and the notion of quality time is a myth. Spending a few "quality" hours with our children is insufficient for good parenting. Children on Israeli kibbutzim (communal settlements) used to be raised in children's houses, spending only an hour or so of "quality time" per day with their parents. Today, such children's houses are a thing of the past on most kibbutzim. Parents realize that quality time demands a quantity of time.

The second journey of life is the journey toward maturity, from indulging to disciplining our appetites. It begins with controlling the *yetzer hara*, the evil inclination, and developing the *yetzer hatov*, the good inclination. It continues with the realization that nothing worthwhile in life comes instantaneously. Those parts of life that provide our deepest fulfillment require huge investments of time, energy and self-discipline.

Living by Rules

A young man, eighteen years old, came to see me. He had grown up in a very strict household with many rules, both religious and secular. Now he was breaking away. He resented all the strictures his parents had laid upon him, but at the same time he felt guilty about not following all the rules.

I explained that breaking away was a natural and inevitable part of growing up. Then I asked him this: "In life you are going to make choices, including the choice whether to seek immediate gratification or to not follow your appetites. Do you think your parents' rules helped you develop the self-discipline to say 'no'?" He looked at me as if a light had gone off in his head: "Rabbi, you're right. I hated the rules, but they taught me self-control." I hope my own children, who are growing up in a fairly strict household, will some day appreciate our rules.

Rabbi David Bockman tells a story he learned from an American Indian elder. The elder was describing his inner struggle: "Inside me are two dogs. One of the dogs is kind and good. The other is mean and evil. The mean dog fights the good dog all the time." When asked which dog wins, he reflected for a moment and replied, "The one I feed the most."

This parable says it all. There are rules about how to live a successful life. These rules feed the good inclination and starve the evil inclination.

Guideposts for Your Second Journey: From Self-Indulgence to Self-Control

1. Learning self-discipline and delayed gratification is one of life's toughest tasks. The lesson begins when you are a child. Parents need to set firm household rules (for example, no television before homework, no snacks before dinner, no outside distractions during family mealtime). Children must learn that temper tantrums and out-of-control anger will be met with time-outs, loss of privileges and more severe punishment. At the same time, generosity,

kindness, self-sacrifice and self-discipline need to be rewarded. The best thing parents can do is model kindness and altruistic behavior for their kids.

2. Learn to say no to yourself. This is one of the great lessons of religion. Jewish tradition is filled with rules, such as dietary laws, that curb the appetite and limit behavior. Other faith traditions have similar rules. Catholics require giving up certain pleasures during Lent. Muslims must abstain from alcohol, Mormons from caffeine. These rules have various explanations, but a key purpose is to teach the art of self-control.

   I suggest you practice an appropriate discipline. If you practice a particular faith, abide by one of its disciplines. If you don't ascribe to any established religion, practice a personal self-discipline (for example, no dessert except on weekends, no cigarettes before 2:00 P.M., no television until after spending time with the children). Self-discipline requires practice.

3. Since the evil inclination is simply our appetites out of control, begin with a self-assessment of your

various appetites—hunger, lust, anger, pride, greed. Do you eat to satisfy hunger? Or is food used to satisfy other nonnutritious needs, such as loneliness or depression? Do you have sex as part of an ongoing relationship with a beloved spouse? Or do you act out of sexual lust? Do you control your anger and use it sparingly when confronted by injustice? Or are you quick to lose your temper with your spouse, children, employees and others you meet? If you feel a rage, can you release it in such a way that it harms no one? (I told a family whose son had difficulty controlling his anger to hang a punching bag in the garage.) Has your pride prevented you from saying you're sorry when appropriate? Is the quest for material goods consuming too much of your energy?

4. Can you take a long-term approach to whatever you desire in life? Can you see the big picture? What do you envision for yourself in five years? What small steps are appropriate to meeting that goal, knowing that the big payoff may be years away? (For example, are there college courses you can take now leading to the degree that is part of

your long-term plan?) Write a list of long-term goals and short-term steps to reach those goals.

5. Take time to study the rules of your particular religious faith. For example, Jews might want to study what the Torah teaches about food, sex, anger, money, and good and evil deeds. Christians might want to turn to their church to learn about good works.

6. Take time to develop the *yetzer hatov*, the good inclination. Bring flowers to a nursing home, visit a shut-in, volunteer for a charity, pay the toll for the stranger in the car behind you, smile and share a compliment with someone you meet. Good deeds have a way of multiplying.

7. To find the balance in life, take time to say yes to yourself. You now know that a lifetime of amusement parks is not the key to happiness. However, an occasional day at an amusement part is vital for diversion, to recharge your battery and simply to have fun. Life is not just delayed satisfaction. Sometimes you need to indulge your immediate appetite. Learn to have fun.

The Ultimate Teacher

Rules are vital in the quest for maturity, but how do we know the rules, the proper path to take? We certainly learn from our parents, our mentors and society, but ultimately we learn from God. God did not put us on earth to flounder without guidance or direction. God communicated rules to us for a successful life. In fact, the communication of rules is part of how God shows His love for His creation.

In this sense, God is like a parent. Good parents do not allow their children to write their own rules, to live with no guidance. In Hebrew, the word for parents is *horim*, from a root meaning "to teach." The Hebrew word *Torah* comes from the same root; *Torah* means "teaching." God is the source of Torah. In an ultimate sense,

God is our Teacher.

Family

The Journey from Loneliness to Love

As he [Abram] was about to enter Egypt, he said to his wife Sarai, I know what a beautiful woman you are.

Genesis 12:11

Of a man who loves his wife as himself, honors her more than himself, guides his sons and daughters in the right path . . . scripture says, "And you shall know your tent shall be at peace" (Job 5:24).

Yebamot 62b

Rabbi Moshe Leib of Sasov taught us how to love. He said, "A peasant taught me what is true love of others. The peasant was sitting in an inn drinking with a companion. Suddenly, he turned to his friend and asked: 'Do you love me?'

"'I love you very much.'

"'If you love me, tell me what gives me pain.'

"'How would I know that?'

"'If you don't know what gives me pain, how can you say you love me?'"

Abraham had been married a number of years, but until he went down to Egypt he and his wife Sarah did not interact much. She came along on their journey, but he hardly seemed to notice her. The Torah records no conversation between them. We do not know how she felt about their travels. All we know about Sarah until she arrived in Egypt is that she was unable to conceive children.

Abraham was concerned about how the Egyptians would treat him and Sarah. Abraham was also concerned that if the Egyptians learned Sarah was his wife they might kill him in order to have her. So he asked her to pretend that she was his sister. Unfortunately, the plan backfired, and she was kidnapped into Pharaoh's harem, where she was held until her true identity became known. When Pharaoh learned that she was a married woman, he returned her to Abraham. (It is interesting to note here that Abraham and Sarah did not learn from this experience; rather, they tried the same scheme later with the pagan king Abimelech. Abraham and Sarah's son, Isaac, and Isaac's Rebecca also tried the same scheme. The same mistakes are made so often from generation to generation.)

The story relates that as Abraham and Sarah approached the border with Egypt, Abraham seemed to see his wife for the first time. The rabbinic midrash asks why did he first mention her beauty then, after all their travels? In general, traveling takes a toll on one's beauty, yet Sarah seemed to grow more beautiful throughout her travels. Nowhere during his journey did Abraham find a woman as beautiful as Sarah (Genesis Rabbah 40:4).

The midrash also states that Abraham tried to hide Sarah as they approached the Egyptian border. He placed her in a box, but the customs inspector stopped him. "You have garments in the box?" he asked.

"I will pay the customs on garments," Abraham replied.

"Perhaps you have silks in the box?"

"I will pay the customs on silks."

"Perhaps you have precious stones in the box?"

"I will pay the customs on precious stones."

Abraham kept upping the price, realizing that what he had in the box was more valuable even than precious stones. "A good wife, who can find, her price is above rubies" (Proverbs 31:10). Finally, Abraham opened the box, and Sarah's beauty shone throughout Egypt (Genesis Rabbah 40:5). For the first time, Abraham truly saw the beauty of his wife and realized what was valuable in his life.

Family as an Ideal

Jewish mystics teach that Adam, the first human created by God, was neither male nor female. He/she was both. When God caused a deep sleep to fall on this first person, God literally split him/her in half, separating the male and the female halves.

This ancient belief teaches that originally the soul was neither male nor female but a combination of both.

Part of our work in life is to find our other half, the one we call our *beshert* (Yiddish for "intended"). The Talmud teaches, "Forty days before the creation of a child, a voice proclaims in heaven so-and-so's daughter for so-and-so's son" (Sotah 2a). The search for a partner has cosmic significance.

Those with a more practical bent would say that we do not have a single *beshert.* Each of us has many potential life partners. Our job is to begin our search for the right one as we take the third great journey of life — the journey from loneliness to love.

Of course, one must be careful when speaking about the journey to family. According to the Torah, marriage and family is certainly a religious ideal. Yet, not everybody will marry or find joy in marriage, and not every marriage will succeed. Not every marriage will be blessed with children. Marriage and children may not be right for everybody, for a variety of reasons, but it is still the dream of most people. We dream of finding our *beshert,* starting a family and growing old together. How can we make that dream come true?

We grow up and leave home. We demonstrate the maturity and self-control necessary to be successful and happy. We have a powerful appetite for sex, which is a fundamental part of our biological nature. We also have a powerful appetite for intimacy and connection. How do we direct these twin drives toward family?

The structure of family goes beyond the biological and material and touches the spiritual dimension of life. In the realm of family life, we rise above our animal nature to touch the godliness within us. Thus does family become a spiritual entity.

Animals live by their instincts, but the Torah asks humans to rise above mere instinct in all family relationships. While most animal parents are finished with their parenting tasks after a relatively brief time, that is not so with human parenting. While humans also have birth mothers and fathers, this biological fact has little to do with parenting, and our parents' tasks are just beginning after birthing and weaning.

Another difference is noted in animals' relationships with their siblings. While animal siblings share genetic material or even the same womb, and while certain species seem to care instinctually for others, no animal has been given the commandment to be their "brother's keeper."

Indeed, animals procreate, and males join sexually

with females and create new generations. Yet this is a totally biological act for animals, with no larger moral or spiritual purpose. In fact, most animals have sexual encounters only when in heat, when fertilization is likely. A male's sperm fertilizes a female's egg and, in most instances, the male then procreates with other females.

Also, following birth and a short period of nursing and nurturing in the animal kingdom, offspring are expected to survive on their own. In very few species can one find the intergenerational ties that characterize human families.

These examples imply that "family" in the animal kingdom is limited to the realm of the biological. For humans, the journey to family is profoundly spiritual. To better understand what this means, let us travel back to the dawn of creation, to that mystical place called the Garden of Eden.

The Garden of Eden

Family life began when God created Adam, placed him in the garden and declared, "It is not good for man to be alone. I will make him a fitting helper" (Genesis 2:18). God brought each animal to Adam, but none was an appropriate helper. Only then did God cause Adam to fall into a deep sleep so He could remove his rib. God created a woman from that rib and declared one of the most important verses in the Torah: "Therefore a man shall leave his mother and father and cleave onto his wife and they shall be one flesh" (Genesis 2:24). No other male in the entire animal kingdom is given that responsibility.

We should note that the Torah does not say, "A man should leave his mother and father for a series of sexual conquests and one-night stands." Sexual discipline stands at the center of the Torah's vision of family life. A human male is not to "scatter his seed" wherever he wishes, although it might be in his genetic self-interest to do so. Nor does the Torah say, "A man shall leave his mother and father and cleave to his wives." Polygamy may have been permitted in biblical times, but it is scarcely the ideal. In fact, one can argue that the biblical stories of Abraham, Sarah and Hagar—or Jacob, Rachel and Leah—are arguments against polygamy. It is noteworthy that all of the great biblical religions have long outlawed polygamy.

Nor does the Torah countenance serial monogamy, one wife after another. Recognizing the reality that marriages do sometimes fail, the Torah does permit divorce (Deuteronomy 24:1–4), though it is considered a sad, last resort when a marriage is irretrievably broken. In fact, the prophet Malachi wrote, "You cover the altar of God with tears, weeping and moaning. . . . Because the Lord is witness between you and the wife of your youth with whom you have broken faith, though she is your partner and covenanted spouse" (Malachi 2:13–14). Based on this verse, the rabbis teach that when a man divorces the wife of his youth, "even the altar of God cries tears" (Gittin 90b).

Lifelong marriage between one man and one woman is the ideal articulated by the Garden of Eden story. Jewish tradition uses the term *kiddushin*, literally "holiness," to describe such a marriage. It is marriage, the commitment of a man and a woman to a lifelong exclusive sexual relationship, that helps us rise above the animal kingdom.

According to the biblical ideal, marriage has two purposes. The first is companionship, for "it is not good for man to be alone" (Genesis 2:18). The second is in order to fulfill God's commandment to "Be fruitful and multiply" (Genesis 1:28). I explore each of these fundamental human commitments in the following pages.

Love and Marriage

Conventional wisdom in contemporary U.S. culture is that we will meet a marriage partner through random chance and we will somehow fall in love. Little girls grow into women who still believe the fairy-tale message, "Someday my prince will come." Men believe in the classic Beatles tune *I Saw Her Standing There* and that they will someday see a woman and know she is "the one." Men and women both believe that this magic called love will carry them through fifty years of successful marriage.

In truth, love alone is not enough. Finding the right marriage partner means making wise choices. It means using one's head, not simply one's heart.

The most important ingredient for a successful marriage is trust, not love. We find someone whose values we share, who has a similar vision of the kind of home they want to build, who attracts us, who makes us feel good about ourselves. Slowly we lower our protective coverings and open our real selves to that individual. This is the purpose of courtship, to use a rather old-fashioned term. Courtship is an attempt to truly know another individual, to gradually uncover our real selves, to open up, to see if we can trust another, to become, as the Bible says of Adam and Eve, "Naked but not ashamed" (Genesis 2:25). The nakedness is not a physical nakedness but a spiritual nakedness, a willingness to allow ourselves to be vulnerable to another. This is the beginning of intimacy.

What is the role of love in creating a successful marriage? The best answer comes out of the Greek view of love. The Greeks had three terms for various aspects of love—*eros, philos and agape. Eros* is romantic love, where sexual attraction is combined with a kind of chemistry. *Philos* is the love that grows out of friendship. It implies an intimacy, a sharing, a total comfort with one another. *Agape* is altruistic love. It is the love the Bible refers to when it speaks of one's soul being bound up in another soul (Genesis 44:30). It is love as service to the other, being and giving for the welfare of the other. It is love built on empathy. It is the love that prompts commitment to a life together.

Real love develops on these three levels—as romance (*eros*), as friendship (*philos*), as service (*agape*). When dating, *eros* is often present early on, while *philos* takes time and trust to develop. It is *agape* that leads to successful marriages. This is the love that Rabbi Moshe of Sasov spoke of when he said, "If you don't know what gives me pain, how can you say you love me?" This is also the lesson from Abraham and Sarah, when Abraham finally took notice of his wife. This is the love we feel when we truly value our partner.

Agape is unconditional: We are there to meet another's needs without expectation of anything in return. The rabbis taught that this unconditional love is the only kind that will last for the long term (Avot 5:20). I am convinced this kind of love does not come to a couple immediately, in the rush of romance. It comes after establishing intimacy, after beginning to build a home together. That is why I tell every couple planning a wedding that true love comes after the marriage.

How does *agape* work in the real world of love and marriage? Perhaps one example from a rather traditional marriage will suffice. A couple came to me for counseling, ready to separate despite their small children. The man had failed in a business venture and was planning to return to school. The couple was struggling financially, and the wife saw the husband as an inadequate breadwinner. Meanwhile, in his struggle to be a provider, the husband was ignoring the wife's needs for intimacy and appreciation.

I asked the woman, "What does your husband truly need? What gives him pain?" I told her that if he was like most men I know, he needed to feel like a winner in her eyes. He needed to feel that she was proud of him for the effort he put into business and that she supported his attempts to be a provider. He needed her admiration.

Then I asked the man, "What does your wife truly need? What gives her pain?" I told him that many marriages begin to unravel when a husband takes his wife for granted. Too many men come home and immediately check the mail, read the newspaper, turn on the computer and ignore their wives. "She needs your appreciation," I said. "She needs touching, intimacy and love."

My advice worked for this couple. Others may have different needs, but a marriage can succeed and flourish when a spouse asks, "What gives my wife/husband pain? How can I meet his/her deepest needs?"

Building a Family

The second purpose of marriage is to bring a new generation into the world. Having children is more than a lifestyle option. In fact, it is the first commandment in the Torah: God told the man He created, "Be fruitful and multiply, fill the earth and subdue it" (Genesis 1:28).

Many would see procreation as the ultimate religious act because in numerous ways we become closer to God when we give birth to a child. As I said in chapter 1, the process of creating a life makes us partners with God and teaches us humility and unselfishness. Parenthood is an act of hope and faith in the future. Having and raising children, the most difficult and the most gratifying choice most people ever make, is a religious vocation.

Our role on earth is to be partners with God in perfecting this world. At no time is that partnership more pronounced than at the birth of a child. A man and a woman have a moment of sexual pleasure, a sperm and an egg find each other, and nine months later a new human being appears. Most people find the moment of birth to be profoundly religious. A popular saying states that there are no atheists in a foxhole—I believe there are no atheists in a delivery room.

If our role on earth is to imitate God, at no time is that more true than when we give birth to a child. Having children is a religious, but also a humbling, experience. Only when we have a child can we approximate how God must have felt when creating Adam and Eve. Only with a child have we created a being over whom we have no control. Our children, so helpless at birth, will grow up and leave the nest; they will make decisions over which we have no power. We create them and let them go. They must forge their own destinies. Somehow, we manage to love them in spite of the choices they make. As the rabbis teach, "A parent's love is toward the child, a child's love is toward his or her child" (Sotah 49a). In this sense, we are like God, who loves His children no matter how far they stray. "As a father has mercy on his children, so God has mercy on those who fear Him" (Psalms 103:13).

Caring for a newborn baby is a totally unselfish act;

we must care for the needs of someone who is totally helpless and cannot return the favor. And there is no guarantee that when that child grows up, he or she will show any appreciation for our effort. Parenthood, more than any other human experience, forces us to give fully to another with no guarantee of a return for our efforts. It makes us overcome the natural human inclination to think, *Me first.*

Having a child is also a demonstration of hope and faith. A classic rabbinic midrash about Miriam, the older sister of Moses, teaches that when Pharaoh decreed to throw all baby boys into the Nile, Moses' parents Amram and Yocheved separated and refused to risk having a baby. Miriam convinced them to come back together. Pharaoh had decreed only against boys, she pointed out, yet her parents' decree was against boys and girls. Pharaoh had decreed it only in this world, but her parents had decreed it against the world to come. Amram and Yocheved came back together, baby Moses was born and the history of the world was changed (Sotah 12a). From this we learn that we should have children despite our concerns about how those children will turn out and that certain matters are best left in the hands of God.

Raising Children

As mentioned earlier, in the animal kingdom the male's job is usually finished following conception. After progeny are born and weaned, the female's job is often finished. Animals leave their forebears, function on their own and the cycle begins again. Not so humans. When we give birth and wean our children, our work is just beginning, which is the other reason the Torah advocates marriage: It is the easiest way to ensure that both a father and a mother are fully present for the difficult task of raising children.

Children have many needs that their parents must meet, often without the expectation of payback or reward. These needs fall into two broad areas, parallel to the first two chapters of this book.

In chapter one, I say that every human being is a unique creation of God and that every human being has his or her own particular mission to accomplish in this world. As a unique creation, all children need the full, unconditional love and acceptance of their parents. Children were not placed in the world to meet their parents' needs. Rather, they are God's creations with their own unique gifts and their own unique purposes.

Most parents claim they love their children. Yet too many have children to fulfill some kind of inner need, to satisfy their own egos or to live out their dreams. Many of the parents I have counseled over the years make a grave mistake: Too often they are more concerned with their own needs than their children's. This is the meaning behind the old joke about the mother who points to her three-year-old and five-year-old children: "This is the doctor and this is the lawyer."

Sometimes parents expect their unfulfilled dreams to be lived out by their children. One of the great Broadway musicals is *Gypsy,* based on the true story of the famous stripper Gypsy Rose Lee. It is really about Gypsy's mother, whose energy was totally focused on fulfilling her own dream through the vaudeville success of her two daughters. In the end, one daughter ran away, and the other became a stripper and declared her independence from her mother. At the end of the story the mother is a sad, bitter woman.

Some parents make the mistake of loving their children because they fulfill some need in them. *Naches* is a good Yiddish word that has come to mean "joy through children." Children become *naches* builders. Too often, parents tend to be focused on their own needs and how their children can meet the requirements of their egos. This was the mistake that Eve, the Bible's first mother, made when she had her first child, Cain. The name Cain comes from the Hebrew word *kana*, "to own or acquire." Eve believed that she now owned a child and that, like all possessions, he was present to meet her needs. One can speculate whether Cain's mother's attitude toward parenting contributed to him growing up to be a murderer.

True parental love focuses not on the needs of the parent but on the needs of the child. It is child-centered rather than parent-centered. True love begins with the questions, "What makes my child distinct and how can I meet the needs of my particular child?" It starts with the theological idea that every child is unique, different from all other humans who have ever or will ever live on this earth. Every child has his or her own mission in life. Children are not on this earth to meet the parents' needs or to fulfill their dreams and desires. Parents do not own their children. On the contrary, parents have been given a sacred trust to guide their children to find their unique paths on this earth. "Guide a son according to *his* way, even when he grows up he will not depart from it" (Proverbs 22:6).

Children have a second fundamental need. In chapter 2, I say that children are born with both an evil inclination *(yetzer hara)* and a good inclination *(yetzer hatov)*. The good inclination is only a potential at birth, the evil inclination is present in full force. Parenting is about teaching children to control the evil inclination and to develop the good inclination. That is why the most important aspect of parenting is teaching. (In Hebrew, the words for teacher and parent come from the same Hebrew root, *hrh*, which is also the root of the word *Torah*, God's teachings to us.)

Teaching is the most difficult aspect of parenting. It involves laying down clear rules of right and wrong, with consequences for infractions. It means consistent punishment for children in order to put them on the right path. Being a parent is different from being a pal. Unfortunately, many parents worry so much about being friends with their children that they neglect the essential discipline necessary to set a child on the right path.

Discipline also means modeling proper behavior. Children learn most by watching what their parents do.

A powerful Hasidic story of the Zhitomer Rabbi tells of him seeing a drunken man staggering in the gutter, with a younger drunken man following him. The younger drunk said to the other, "Dad, wait for me," whereupon the rabbi turned to his son and said, "I envy that father. He has accomplished his goal of having a son like himself. I don't know whether you will be like me. I can only hope that the drunkard is not more successful in training his son than I am with you."

Some parents worry that if they are too strict their children will not love them. I teach a class of teens in my synagogue. Each year I say to them, "Tell me how you would feel if one day your parents said, 'I trust you. There are no more rules. Do what you think is right. Go to bed when you want. Watch whatever movies you want. Eat what you want. Go to school only if you want to. You set the rules.'" At first, most teens love the idea. After a little consideration, they usually reply, "If my parents did that, I would think they did not love me."

Children need rules. They must develop discipline and self-control, vital skills if they are to become successful adults. Once children have been taught the right path, parents have to let them go.

An inevitable fact of parenthood is that children grow up and leave, and parents face an empty nest. Parents must once again turn to each other for companionship and friendship. They must learn to become lovers again, not merely parents. They must live for themselves and for their partners, not just for their children. In becoming lovers, they can turn for wisdom to the One Whom the Bible considers the ultimate lover.

Guideposts for Your Third Journey: From Loneliness to Love

1. Family begins when each of us searches for someone else to love and someone to love us. If you are beginning that search, you need to make physical, financial, emotional and spiritual preparations. Physical preparation includes proper diet, exercise, grooming and dress. Financial preparation means finding a way to contribute to the support of a household. Emotional preparation means healing wounds

from previous relationships, perhaps with the help of a professional counselor. Spiritual preparation means developing the right attitude toward dating, knowing that you are searching for a life partner and not merely a casual date or sexual liaison. You must turn inward before turning outward.

2. In our society, we need to replace recreational dating with courtship, the gradual uncovering of yourself to another human being as he or she uncovers himself or herself to you. You need to learn about the other's values—kindness, honesty, even-temperedness, patience. For example, how do they treat subordinates—a waitress in a restaurant, a shopkeeper, their employees? What are their feelings about family, religion, money, children, sex, gender roles? Each of these issues can make or break a marriage.

3. Most people date looking for love, but love ought to be last on your list. First, seek trust, intimacy, communication, shared values, physical attraction, friendship. With these pieces in place, love can grow.

4. Too often people put the effort into the courtship before the marriage. Once marriage takes place, it

is easy to take the relationship for granted. Marriage, like all physical systems, will wind down unless infused with energy. Married couples need a regular date night, preferably weekly. They also need time away from home and children, time with each other, preferably several times a year. A baby-sitter is cheaper than a marriage counselor.

5. Take time to notice, love, appreciate, compliment and value your partner. My counseling experience has taught me that women in particular view success in terms of relationships. A wife needs to hear from her husband that she is absolutely precious in his eyes.

6. Admire and be proud of your partner. People want to feel like winners, particularly in the eyes of those closest to them. My counseling experience has taught me that men in particular view success in terms of achievement. A husband needs to hear the words "I love you," but perhaps more important, he needs to hear the words "I am proud of you."

7. The people we love need our time. Children in particular need quantity time, not simply quality time, with their parents. Take your child on a one-on-one vacation. Bring him or her on a business trip. I still

have vivid memories of a business trip with my father when I was fifteen years old. It brought me much closer to my him during a difficult time in my life. Put your children to bed each night with a set ritual. Set aside times to be with one another.

8. Children must receive unconditional love and be valued for their uniqueness. They must also be taught right and wrong, self-discipline, and delayed gratification. The best way to teach is to be a constant presence in their lives. Teach by example.

9. Children need a lot of attention, but eventually they grow up and leave. A couple is left with one another. My wife and I keep a sign up in our kitchen that says, "The best thing a father can do for his children is love their mother." The converse is also true: "The best thing a mother can do for her children is love their father."

The Meaning of Love

One book in the Bible is especially deeply surprising to the casual reader. It is called "Song of Songs," or sometimes "Song of Solomon." It is highly erotic, describing a loving and often sexual relationship between a young shepherd girl and her lover.

The rabbis engaged in much debate about whether such a book was appropriate for the holy canon. Rabbi Akiba argued that Song of Songs was the holiest book of them all (Yadayim 3:5) for the book is a metaphor: The shepherd girl is the people Israel, her lover is God. Despite many temptations, including being taken into the harem of the wealthy king, the shepherd girl ultimately remains faithful to her lover.

The great philosopher Martin Buber taught that when we fully relate to the one whom we love, we catch a glimpse of God. He called such relationships I-Thou. I-Thou is a total relationship between two human beings. It is nonutilitarian, self-enhancing, almost timeless. An I-Thou relationship has a spiritual dimension. To Buber, it is only in such relationships that we come to know God. "Every particular I-Thou is a glimpse through to the Eternal Thou" (Buber, 1958). Such relationships lift our lives beyond a mundane, animal existence and allow us to be attuned to our Creator. Such I-Thou relationships are what most of us have in mind when we speak of love. Through our meeting the needs of another, we ultimately realize that

God is our Lover.

4

Prosperity

The Journey from Sustenance to Abundance

Now Abram was very rich in cattle, silver and gold.

Genesis 13:2

There are four types of people (regarding money). One who says, "What is mine is mine, what is yours is yours." This is a mediocre person. Some say this is the way of Sodom. One who says, "What is mine is yours, what is yours is mine." This is an ignoramus. One who says, "What is mine is yours, what is yours is yours." This is a pious person. One who says, "What is yours is mine, what is mine is mine." This is a wicked person.

Avot 5:14

There was a rabbi, a great scholar and sage, who filled his whole life with acts of piety. He knew that he would be justly rewarded in the world to come. So he prayed to God to let him see who would sit next to him in the next world, who would be his study partner. And God granted him his wish.

God took him to a little shop where a poor shoe-maker slaved away. All day and far into the night the man made shoes, and yet he seemed to have little to show for it. The shop was poor. The man never took time to study. He badly needed to bathe and change his clothes. The rabbi was outraged. "O God, after all my acts of piety, this man is to be my neighbor and study partner! What kind of justice is this?" God answered, "Go talk to the shoemaker."

The rabbi introduced himself. The shoemaker answered, "I have heard of your great piety. I wish I had time to learn with you. But who has the time? All day I work hard to make shoes for the rich; they pay my living. And then, when there is leather left over, all night I work hard to make shoes for the poor. Nobody should be without shoes because they cannot afford them." The rabbi turned to God.

*"Ribono Shel Olam, Master of the World, I am not
worthy to sit with him."*

The journey from mere sustenance to prosperity is
the fourth great journey of life. Each of us must ask
these questions at some time: How will I provide for
myself and my family? What will I do in order to provide? What is to be my attitude toward wealth and
money?

Events occur in the ancient story of Abraham that
illustrate this journey, events that are often repeated in
our own society. It becomes clear that wealth can create
dissension within a family.

After reconciling the incident that took place
between his wife, Sarah, and Pharaoh, king of Egypt,
Abraham developed a profitable business relationship
with Pharaoh. By the time he returned to Canaan,
Abraham was a well-established and wealthy shepherd
with huge flocks and much gold and silver.

Abraham's nephew Lot, who had traveled to Egypt
with him, also prospered there. However, that prosperity, which resulted in flocks that were too large for the
land to support, prevented him from staying with

Abraham. The family business that Abraham and Lot had built up together had to be split up.

Abraham told Lot to pick the direction he would travel so he could go in the opposite direction. "If you go to the right, I will go to the left; if you go to the left, I will go to the right" (Genesis 13:9). Lot chose to leave his uncle, move east and settle in the city of Sodom.

Sodom was a city known for the selfishness of its residents, a place where people did not comprehend the proper role of money. A powerful symbolism is present in Lot's move toward Sodom, as I will show later in this chapter.

Who Will Provide?

A woman brings her fiancé home to meet her parents. He is a biblical scholar who has dedicated his life to the study of God's law. The parents ask the young man, "How will you provide for our daughter?"

"I plan to dedicate my life to studying the Bible and its commentaries. I am a religious man. I know that God will provide."

The father responds, "Okay, you have my blessing to marry our daughter."

His wife shrieks, "How can you do that? This man can't earn a living!"

The father answers, "He called me God."

I have heard this story told by both Jews and Christians, so it must reflect an attitude that is as popular as it is false. Many of us believe that God will provide for all our needs. Though it is true that God in some ultimate sense is our provider, to use an old cliché, God helps those who help themselves. We are meant to be partners with God in providing for ourselves and our families.

I meet people on a regular basis who believe that God will provide. They come by my office in the synagogue asking for handouts. I do maintain a small charity fund for people who are truly down on their luck, and I will give emergency money for those in need. What bothers me is able-bodied people capable of providing for themselves who constantly come back for handouts without seeking a job. I have often told a person, "Go home and shower, put on clean clothes, walk the mall and find somebody to give you a job." They are painful words. I want to provide for people's emergency needs. However, I do not wish to be an enabler, allowing people to avoid the responsibility of holding down a job and providing for themselves and their families.

In chapter one, I wrote about the responsibility of a child to leave home and seek economic independence. However, I meet some people who believe their parents will provide forever. They live at home into their thirties and forties, enjoying the largesse of their mother and father, despite the Talmud teaching that a man must teach his son a trade so he can earn a living. "Rabbi Judah taught, 'Whoever does not teach his son a trade, it is as if he has taught him to be a thief'" (Kiddushin 29a).

I meet some people who believe that society ought to provide. Actually, this is simply the secular version of the teaching that God will provide. Certainly, society has a responsibility to ensure that people who are down and out have their basic physical needs cared for, to provide a safety net. At the same time, the highest level of giving is helping someone become self-sufficient and self-supporting. The ultimate goal is for everyone to provide for themselves and their family.

The words "God will provide" may be true in the animal kingdom, where most animals seem to find in nature what they need to survive. Perhaps it was true in the Garden of Eden, where all Adam and Even had to do was pick the fruit of the nearest tree. After all, in the Garden they were animal-like, "naked and not ashamed" (Genesis 2:25). However, unless we choose to live in the woods, seeking caves for shelter and picking berries to eat, we must go out into society and provide for ourselves and our families.

At the dawn of creation, God expelled humans, the parents of all humanity, from the Garden of Eden. God said, "By the sweat of your brow will you eat bread" (Genesis 3:19). Since that time, the world has no longer provided us a living.

As someone who must earn a living for myself, my wife and our three children, I know there are few acts more difficult than providing for the needs of one's family. Therefore, we do well to recognize providing for what it is: an act of love.

The Bible tells that Jacob deeply loved his cousin Rachel. He sought her hand in marriage and was told by her father that he must work seven years for her. The

Bible records how the time flew: "They seemed like a few days because of his love for her" (Genesis 29:20). In the end, he worked fourteen years for her, all out of love.

We live in an age where going to work is a high-pressure, high-risk activity. We are held to performance standards and risk losing our jobs if we do not meet these standards. There is little loyalty, whether from supervisors, clients or customers. In an age of corporate downsizing and business bankruptcies, we are always at risk of losing a job. We are judged not by our humanity, but by our ability to perform a task, make the sale, meet the quota, find the client. If we fail to perform, we lose our livelihood.

Yet most of us show up year in and year out, despite the difficulty of our work, because we realize that it is our responsibility. What we don't always understand or remember is that working to provide is an act of love.

Men feel particular pressure to be providers for their families. Often their sense of self-worth is dependent upon their success as providers. As I mention in chapter 3, I see that marriages often begin to falter because the man has failed as a provider and lost the respect of his wife. When men fail as providers, they will often pursue other means by which to build up their self-worth. Alcoholism, adultery and abuse—the "three a's"—are often the path they choose.

Women, whether by choice or necessity, also feel great pressure today to help provide for their families. Sometimes they are abandoned by men and forced by circumstances to provide for themselves and their children. Sometimes the very cost of a middle-class lifestyle necessitates a two-income family. The modern feminist movement too often makes women feel inadequate if they choose not to pursue a career and share the burden of providing.

Providing for a family is more than a necessity. It is an act of love. Now and again we need to hear, "Thank you for providing for us," from our loved ones. Providing is an act that too often is unappreciated in our society.

Each of us needs to ask ourselves, "How will I provide for myself and my family? How will I earn the necessary wages and salary so that I do not become dependent on the largesse of others, whether parents, other family members or society as a whole?" Each married couple needs to see themselves as an economic unit and ask how will they support themselves in their marriage. The cliché, "Love will provide," is as dangerous as it is false; it is often economic problems that mark the beginning of the breakdown of a marriage.

As we work to provide for ourselves and our families, we also ought to recognize the danger of overwork, of living simply to earn a paycheck. Do we live to work, or do we work to live? There must be a limit of providing.

The Limits of Providing

My parents' generation emphasized being a provider. My father considered himself a "good family man." To my father, that meant that he provided for his family. For most men and many women of that generation, being a good provider was the ultimate act of love. When I conduct funerals for men in my father's generation, I often hear these words from children of the deceased: "He was a good man. He took care of our mother and us."

My generation emphasizes finding the limits of providing. If providing is an act of love, perhaps the more we work and the more we provide, the more this shows our love. The Ten Commandments disagree—they call for a limit on providing and define a cycle of work and rest. We are commanded to spend time at our place of employment and to balance that with time spent at home with our families. As I often tell overstressed parents who come to see me, "Your children need your presence rather than your presents." Our families need us in our lives.

At the urging of his wife, a busy businessman finally takes a day off from work to take their young son fishing. The father and son spend the entire day together, although the father frets about what he is missing at the office. At the end of the day, the father writes in his calendar, "Took my son fishing; wasted the whole day." Meanwhile, the son writes in his diary, "My dad took me fishing; the greatest day of my life."

Wisdom resides in the ability to draw limits. It is the ability to find a rhythm between work and rest, between job time and family time, though different people may understand the requirement of rest differently.

In the animal world, one day is like every other. For humans, a weekly Sabbath is one way to rise above the animal world. However we choose to observe our Sabbath, we should remember that when we were slaves in Egypt we worked seven days per week. Every day was like every other. When we won our freedom, we had to learn to draw a line and stop our work, to find rest and discover family time.

The cycle of work and rest requires more than merely going home from a job. Rest also means leaving our work at work. It means turning off the pagers and voice mail, the fax machines and e-mail, which keep us forever connected to the office. Rabbi Jack Riemer tells a beautiful story about this:

> *As he comes home from the office each evening, a man stops at a tree in front of his house. He touches the branches and walks into his home. Each morning he touches the branches again before leaving for work. His neighbor asks him, "What are you doing?" The man answers, "This is my worry tree. Each evening I hang all of my worries from work on the branches. I do not bring them into the house. The next morning I take them back to work. But they seem so much lighter the next morning."*

We need to rest for ourselves, as well as for our families. At work, we are judged by our performance. We are valued not by who we are but by what we accomplish. Accomplishment and success are important to our egos, but it is difficult to always be on call, to always be judged by what we do. We need time simply to be.

At home we are not judged for what we do. As I note in the previous chapter, true love is unconditional. We are loved simply for being, not for any of our accomplishments. When our children hug us after work, it is not because we received a promotion or reached performance expectations or brought in a new client or made the sale. At home we can simply be. The pattern of sacred rest gives us time to stop doing and, simply, to be.

Four Attitudes Toward Money

Bernard Baruch told a story about his father that offers us a profound insight about money:

Baruch was a great financier, an advisor to presidents, with a deep understanding of the stock market. As a young man, he made one million dollars and wanted to

share the news with his father. He phoned him and said,
"Father, I made my first million." He expected his father
to share his excitement and enthusiasm.

His father was silent for a long time. At last he
said, "Bernard, what are you going to do with it?"
All his life he remembered those words, and he
repeated them over and over. It is not enough to earn
the money. What are we going to do with it that will
make a difference?

As we go out into the world of business and work to
provide for our families, much of our success depends
upon our attitudes toward money. The famous passage
from the Talmud quoted at the beginning of this chapter describes four approaches toward money. Let us
explore these four attitudes in reverse order, from lowest
to highest importance.

The Avaricious Mindset

"'What is yours is mine, what is mine is mine.' This is
a wicked person." Some people are never satisfied with
what they have. They try to seize the property of their
fellow human beings.

The Talmud teaches, "Who is rich? Whoever is satisfied with their portion" (Avot 4:1). Unfortunately, some people are never satisfied. It often begins with coveting the possessions of our fellow humans, a desire forbidden by the last of the Ten Commandments. Eventually it may involve cheating or even stealing to acquire illegitimately that which belongs to others.

The Torah is filled with laws forbidding activities to acquire another's property in an illegitimate manner. "You shall not steal; you shall not deal deceitfully or falsely with one another" (Leviticus 19:11). "You shall not defraud your neighbor. You shall not commit robbery. The wages of a laborer shall not remain with you until morning" (Leviticus 19:13). "You shall not falsify measures of length, weight or capacity. You shall have an honest balance, honest weights, an honest *ephah* and honest *hin*" (Leviticus 19:35–36).

In the Bible, the penalty for stealing is to return the stolen object, together with a fine equal to the amount stolen. "He [the thief] must make restitution; if he lacks the means, he shall be sold for his theft. But if what he stole . . . be found alive in his possession, he shall pay double" (Exodus 22:2–4).

However, if the thief steals oxen or sheep and slaughters them, he shall pay four or five times the value of the animal. Why is the penalty so much harsher for oxen and sheep? One must remember that these biblical laws developed during a historical period when the Israelites were shepherds. By stealing and slaughtering animals, thieves were literally taking away their victims' livelihoods. If the highest form of charity is to help someone earn a living, the lowest form of stealing is to prevent someone from earning a living.

This is reflected in numerous Torah laws. It is forbidden to remove someone's landmark (Deuteronomy 27:17). Later rabbinic law interpreted this as a prohibition on unfair competition, deliberately trying to force someone out of business (Baba Batra 21b). A lender cannot take the millstone as pledge on a loan to someone who owns a mill because the worst form of thievery is to steal someone else's livelihood.

God created a world in which there is enough wealth to go around without having to steal what belongs to others. I remember counseling an accountant who debated whether or not to hold on to his job. His employer was asking him to keep a false set of books in order to fool government regulators. Ultimately, his employers were asking him to steal from the public, as well as risk his professional reputation. The job was a good-paying one, and the man had a family to support.

I told him that each morning he had to wake up and look in the mirror. Did he like the man he saw? Ultimately, his good name was more important for his children than any salary he brought home. I was pleased when he resigned from that position and looked for a more honorable employer.

The Idealistic Mindset

"'What is mine is yours, what is yours is mine.' This is an ignoramus." Many idealistic people see the solution to inequalities of wealth in the removal of private property altogether. "Let everybody work for everybody; what is mine is yours and vice versa. Let us all work for the common good and share our income with one another." As Karl Marx put it, "From each according to his ability, to each according to his needs."

In theory it sounds wonderful. In practice, history has shown that it does not work. In Communist Russia, such socialism was the basis of an entire society. It led to corruption, inefficiency and eventually the breakdown of an entire economy.

Such an idealistic view of money may work in smaller, self-selecting communities. Families function by sharing financial resources among family members. The kibbutz in Israel was founded on shared wealth, with everybody working for the common good and sharing property. Today, even kibbutzniks are discovering that humans beings may work hard for themselves and their immediate families but, unless they are extremely idealistic, they are less likely to work hard for the common good.

My oldest friend learned this lesson the hard way. He was part of a communal village in Israel, with all salaries going into a common fund and each family drawing equally. This extremely idealistic form of economy lasted only a few years. Soon, anger and resentment entered communal life. People felt that others were not carrying their full weight; some were drawing benefits without contributing as much as they were capable to the common good. Eventually the village restructured its entire economy, with each family keeping its own salary and paying taxes for common needs.

Socialist approaches to wealth fail because they do not consider the reality of human nature. As I note in chapter two, we humans have a *yetzer hara* (an evil inclination) and a *yetzer hatov* (a good inclination), and we will do whatever is necessary to fulfill our own appetites. Working for the common good does not come naturally. A more realistic approach is to encourage individuals to provide for themselves and their families and to accumulate as much wealth as possible. Only then can they learn to share what they have acquired through their own hard work.

The Scarcity Mindset

"'What is mine is mine, what is yours is yours.' This is a mediocre person. Some say this is the way of Sodom." The Torah describes the destruction of the evil cities of Sodom and Gemorrah. What was so evil about these two cities? The rabbis teach that their evil ways were based on their attitudes toward money.

The people of Sodom hoarded their money. When Abraham's nephew Lot moved into town, they welcomed him. He was a wealthy man, and they saw an economic advantage in having him as a neighbor. However, poor people, beggars and visitors without money to spend were not welcome in Sodom.

According to the rabbinic midrash, when a certain poor man came into town a young woman was kind to him and shared her money. When the people heard this, they attacked and tortured her (Sanhedrin 109b). Helping the poor, they believed, would set a bad precedent for the community; beggars and poor people would move into town. The Torah teaches that "God heard her cry" (Genesis 18:21), the cry of a generous young woman attacked by her wicked neighbors.

The people of Sodom had a scarcity complex. They believed there was only so much wealth to go around and that if people shared money each would have less. This scarcity attitude toward money leads to people hoarding and being selfish. That was the mistake of Sodom, and the mistake of too many selfish individuals today. That is why the Torah tries to inculcate in us humans a prosperity mindset that sees wealth as ever-expanding and the sharing of wealth as leading to abundance.

The Prosperity Mindset

The Sodom and Gemorrah story teaches us to have a different attitude about money—to believe that wealth is to be shared and passed on: "'What is mine is yours, what is yours is yours.' This is a pious person." Or, as a Buddhist leader taught, "Money is round so that it will keep rolling." Many great teachers have taught that when we share our wealth, our charity comes back to bless us and we receive more in return.

A poor groom was given a very generous wedding gift, an envelope containing two hundred rubles. The benefactor told him to buy a business in order to support his new wife and future family.

After the wedding festivities were over, the groom walked through the marketplace searching for an appropriate business. He came upon a spice shop that seemed busy with customers. The proprietor was willing to sell it for two hundred rubles. The young newlywed reached into his pocket for the money and discovered that the envelope was missing. His eyes filled with tears as he ran blindly from the store.

The young man ran into a well-dressed man who

*extended his hand to him. "Why are you crying?"
the older man asked. The young man spilled out the
story of the missing envelope.*

*The well-dressed man responded, "I found a
bundle of two hundred rubles a short time ago. I
took the money to my house for safekeeping until I
could find the owner. Tell me, what denomination
were the bills so I can be sure they are yours?"*

"My bundle had forty-five ruble notes."

*"That is exactly what I found. Wait a moment
while I run home."*

*The well-dressed man returned a few moments
later and handed the young groom two hundred
rubles. Smiling, the groom left to buy the business.*

*The well-dressed man did not know that, hidden
in the shadows, the thief was watching the whole
time. The thief approached the well-dressed man
and said, "I confess. I am the one who stole the
money from that young man. I feel terrible. Let me
pay you back."*

*The well-dressed man responded, "I don't want
the money. You have already stolen once. Do not
steal my opportunity to perform a good deed or*

deprive me of the blessing I will receive." With those words, he walked away (Adapted from Labovitz, 1990, p. 118).

Numerous times during my career, someone successful in business has spoken to me about their success. "Rabbi, a few years ago I went through a very hard time. I do not know how we survived financially. However, we decided that we would continue to make our donations and support worthy causes. Whatever little money came in, we always gave something back to the community. I am convinced that our giving led directly to our success today."

Rather than a scarcity paradigm (wealth is limited and the more I give away, the less I have), we ought to live by the prosperity paradigm: Wealth is unlimited. If one person has more, it does not mean that someone else has less. Because Bill Gates is a multibillionaire does not mean that the rest of us are poorer. (If anything, his wealth has created more wealth.)

The biblical lesson is that we live in a world of unlimited wealth, and that wealth is given to us with the condition that we constantly give some away. The biblical ideal prompts us to move from a scarcity paradigm to a prosperity paradigm, to recognize that God created a world filled with almost unlimited opportunities to successfully provide for ourselves and our families.

Guideposts for Your Fourth Journey: From Sustenance to Abundance

1. The journey to prosperity begins with a candid financial self-evaluation. A financial or vocational advisor can be a huge help. What are your assets? What are your liabilities?
2. What do you need to adequately provide for your material needs? What are necessities and what are simply luxuries?
3. Who will work outside the home in your family? You? Your spouse? Both? Your children?

The self-evaluation continues with serious career questions.

4. How will you earn a living? What kind of educational credentials does this career require? What other skills should you learn? Computers?

Bookkeeping? A foreign language? Sales? Management? How can you realistically receive the necessary credentials for this career?

5. Develop a reputation of absolute honesty and integrity in your business and financial dealings. Do not trade short-term gains for long-term loss of reputation. The material world rewards honesty, integrity, consistency and reliability.

6. How can you find joy in the world of work? Sometimes in order to succeed at a task, we have to see the bigger picture.

> *Two bricklayers were asked, "What do you do?" The first said, "All day long, layer after layer, I lay down bricks." The second replied, "All day long, layer after layer, I build skyscrapers." Which bricklayer receives more joy at work?*

7. In counseling people about their careers, I encourage them to give me what some would call an "elevator speech" (see chapter 1). You are in an elevator on the fifth floor, traveling down to the first floor, and you have just a few moments to describe to a stranger what you do for a living.

What would you say? Now suppose you are in the same elevator, and you must describe your life's mission. The task is this: How can these two be brought together?

8. Make one day in seven a day of rest. You may want to study the traditions of your particular religious faith regarding the Sabbath. Or, you may want to develop your own rules. I recommend certain strict rules of separation from the weekday—beginning with not conducting business or earning a livelihood on that day. The day could also include prayer, family meals, recreation, an afternoon nap and private time. Take a walk, go to the beach, read a novel or play games. What is vital is that on this day you stop doing and simply be.

9. When you receive your paycheck, pay yourself first. Put a percentage of every paycheck into a savings plan or investment instrument for yourself and your family.

10. Pay the world second. Give something from each paycheck to worthy causes and charities. The biblical standard of tithing is 10 percent of gross income.

11. The highest level of giving is helping another person provide for himself. Support small businesses and entrepreneurs you admire, even if the big chains sell it cheaper. Be a generous tipper for quality service. Help others earn a living.

12. View the world as a place that allows you to prosper. Go out each day with a prosperity mindset. See yourself as financially successful. Motivational speakers have taught the importance of visualizing what you desire—envision it in your mind and it will come true.

A World of Wealth

To see the world as a place of wealth and prosperity involves a certain mindset. It was the mindset that allowed so many immigrants to come to America dirt poor and work hard with the dream that their families would be better off someday. It is a mindset filled with hope for a brighter future.

God created a world that allows us to prosper while fulfilling our tasks. We can do what we are meant to do while bringing in what we need to take care of ourselves and our families.

We live in a world where we need to work hard to provide for ourselves and our families. We also live in a world that allows us to prosper and succeed. We need to consider everything we earn as a gift from God and to be prepared to give some of it away so others can succeed. We work hard for our wealth, but in an ultimate sense

God is our Provider.

5

Anatomy

The Journey from Frailty to Health

*W*hen Abram heard that his kinsman had been taken captive, he mustered his army, born into his household, numbering three hundred and eighteen, and went in pursuit as far as Dan.

Genesis 14:14

*P*raised are You, Lord our God, King of the Universe, Who has created mankind with wisdom, making many holes and tubes. It is known before Your holy throne that should one of these be blocked when it should be open, or be open when it should be blocked, we could not exist before You. Praised are You Lord, healer of flesh, Who does wonderful things.

Morning Prayer

Once when he was finishing his studies, the elder Hillel walked with his students beside him. The students said to him, "Master, where are you going?" He answered, "To perform a religious duty." "What is this religious duty?" "I am going to wash in the bathhouse." "That is a religious duty?" his disciples queried. "Yes," Hillel replied. "If the statues of the Roman emperors, which are erected in theaters and circuses, are scoured and washed, how much more so should I, created in the image of the Almighty, wash myself" (Leviticus Rabbah 34:3).

Abraham was a middle-aged man, settled into his professional and family life. Suddenly a drastic change in his life occurred. A great war had broken out, which the Bible refers to as the war of the four kings against the war of the five kings. The king of Sodom was pulled into the war, and Abraham's nephew Lot was kidnapped.

Abraham and Lot had fought over money, and each had gone his separate way. Still, Abraham knew he had a familial responsibility to his nephew, and that he must muster the troops of his household and persuade his followers to go to war to rescue his nephew.

Previous family conflicts had to be set aside.

Abraham the shepherd now became Abraham the soldier. He found himself in the field fighting a bitter enemy. The physical had suddenly become important. Abraham had to put his body to the test. He and his soldiers defeated the enemy kings and rescued Lot and the other captives. The soldiers tried to reward Abraham, but he refused them. He had not gone to war to be enriched but to rescue his nephew.

According to a rabbinic midrash, the soldiers tried to make Abraham into a god (Genesis Rabbah 42:5). This followed the pattern of many kings and generals in the ancient world, who began to see themselves as divine. Abraham, despite his victory, realized that he was not a god but a mortal human being in a body that would not live forever.

How different was Abraham from Pharaoh, king of Egypt, who lived several generations later. Pharaoh actually saw himself as a god. A well-known midrash asks how Pharaoh happened to be down by the Nile River early in the morning when Moses met him and threatened to turn the Nile to blood. The answer begins with the fact that Pharaoh tried to pose as a god. He did not want people to believe that he had bodily needs like everybody else. So early each morning he would sneak out of his palace to take care of his needs by the Nile before others were awake. Moses, who knew of Pharaoh's habit, was waiting for him there (Exodus Rabbah 9:8).

Moses meeting Pharaoh provided proof that Pharaoh was not a god. He was a human being with a human body. Our bodies make us mortal. How we treat and understand ourselves as physical beings is the fifth great journey of life.

The Meaning of Our Bodies

The Torah teaches that "God formed man from the dust of the earth, and He breathed into his nostrils the breath of life, and man became a living being" (Genesis 2:7), a statement that names the two aspects of our existence as humans. First, we carry the breath of God (the Hebrew word for soul, *neshama*, literally means "breath"); we are spiritual beings. Part of us is eternal and unchanging. We have a soul, and it is the soul that connects us to that part of the universe that is eternal. Second, we are formed from the dust of the earth. We are physical, material beings, subject to the natural laws of physics and biology. Like all physical entities, our bodies wear down and eventually die. According to the scientific law of entropy, all physical things eventually fall apart or, as W. B. Yeats wrote so powerfully in his poem *The Second Coming*:

> *Turning and turning in the widening gyre*
> *The falcon cannot hear the falconer;*
> *Things fall apart; the centre cannot hold.*

According to scientists, some day the sun will run out of fuel, and in fact, one day the entire universe will die. We humans are material beings who live in a physical world. Eventually we too will die. Our mortality is part of what sets us apart from God, Who is immortal. The way we relate to our material bodies is linked to how we relate to God.

A fascinating ruling in the codification of rabbinic law focuses on torts, or damages. If someone says to another person, "Destroy my property and you will not be liable," the person who destroys the property is not liable. However, even if someone says, "Injure my body and you will not be liable," the person who damages the body is held liable (Baba Kamma 8:7). The logic in that ruling is that we may relieve someone of responsibility for damages to our property. We own it and are free to do whatever we want with it. However, we are not free to relieve someone of responsibility for damage to our bodies because *we do not own our bodies.* This is a profound religious idea. We occupy our bodies, and we are responsible for the maintenance and well-being of our bodies while we are living. But ultimately our bodies belong not to us but to God. They are given to us on loan.

This same principle is seen in another biblical law: "You shall not make gashes in your flesh for the dead, or incise any marks on yourself: I am the Lord" (Leviticus 19:28). Tattoos, for example, are explicitly forbidden in the Torah. The question is why?

Imagine leasing a home. If you buy the home, you are free to paint it any color and decorate it any way you want, as long as you obey local zoning laws. But if you lease a home, it remains someone else's property, and you are allowed only the normal wear and tear of living in the home. You are not permitted to make any permanent marks.

Our bodies are like that leased home. We are temporary occupants. Ultimately, our bodies belong to God. When our time of occupation is finished, we give them back to God as undamaged as possible. This theological idea has powerful implications for how we live our lives.

Whatever the value of the popular feminist text *Our Bodies, Ourselves,* the title is foreign to the biblical vision. We have use of our bodies but they do not belong to us. That gives us a sacred responsibility to treat our physical selves as loans from God. At the least, we need to ensure that our bodies have adequate nutrition, exercise, sleep, medical care and minimal stress. We want to keep that body as healthy as we can.

In addition, when we need to decide about such difficult ethical issues as abortion, euthanasia, experimental medical procedures or self-sacrifice to save others, we begin with the notion that our bodies are on loan. We cannot say, "It is my body and I will do whatever I want." This may profoundly influence how we deal with all of these controversial religious issues. Viewing our bodies as being on loan from God gives us a strong religious sense of how to deal with some of life's most perplexing ethical questions.

Caring for the Body

Our bodies are machines composed of the dust of the earth. In fact, they are complex organisms that are finely tuned to function in the world, absorbing raw material, converting it to energy, eliminating waste, fulfilling our functions and reproducing new generations. Like any fine machine, our bodies need regular and proper maintenance. Most of us know the basics about the food our bodies need to function, the exercise they need to work at maximum efficiency, the sleep they need to repair themselves, and the regular medical checkups needed to ensure ourselves that everything is working properly and that there are no serious diseases or problems.

The knowledge is certainly available in countless books, articles, and Web sites, and from health-care professionals, nutritionists, fitness experts and a variety of other sources. Unfortunately, most of us are far more

careful about the care of our automobiles and the maintenance of our homes than of the bodies we have been
given. Too many of us, myself included, eat too much
or eat the wrong foods, fail to exercise, lack sleep, have
bad habits such as smoking or drinking, allow stress to
overtake us, and ignore the very warning signs our bodies send to the brain that something is not working
properly.

Why is it so easy to ignore the basic maintenance
needs of our body? In chapter two I spoke about the two
forces within our psyche, the *yetzer hara* (evil inclination) and the *yetzer hatov* (good inclination). The evil
inclination is really our appetites out of control. The
good inclination begins with controlling our appetites
and delaying gratification. Nowhere is this need for self-
control more evident than in the day-to-day maintenance of our bodies.

It is always easier to overeat, to avoid exercise, to stay
up too late, and to indulge in too much tobacco or too
many drinks. It is much harder to train ourselves to say
no. Even many highly trained athletes who depend on
their bodies to perform show up at training camp out of
shape. It is a universal human failing. That is why the

rabbis teach the story of the great sage Hillel that I shared at the beginning of this chapter (Leviticus Rabbah 34:3). If the statues of the Roman emperor are properly cared for, how much more so should our bodies—created in God's image—be cared for?

Proper care of the body is one of those areas in which small actions, both good and bad, quickly turn into habits. Habits quickly become part of our character. The rabbis teach that the evil inclination begins as a spiderweb and soon becomes a strong rope (Genesis Rabbah 22:6). Poor habits regarding our body quickly become second nature, making them very difficult to change.

How can we take better care of our bodies? It begins with the realization that our bodies do not belong to us but are gifts from God. The blessing at the beginning of this chapter thanks God for the various openings and tubes in our bodies. If a part of us that should have been opened is closed or vice versa, we could not survive. Traditional Jews say this blessing whenever they meet their bodily needs. I remember saying it with a man after bypass surgery that opened up the blood flow to his heart. He said the words and then broke into tears. It took this serious surgery for him to realize that the proper functioning of his body was a gift from God.

If we think of our bodies as something we lease temporarily, something belonging to God, something to be returned in the best shape possible, we are more apt to treat them properly. That faith can strengthen the good inclination and help bring our appetites under control. As someone who loves food and too often avoids exercise, I can attest that self-care is one of the hardest struggles in the journey to good health.

A Perfect Body

I want to share with you another classic midrash about Abraham. When Abraham's son Isaac was born, God made him look precisely like Abraham. Both Abraham and Isaac had the same features, and they appeared to be around the same age.

Abraham complained to God: "We look alike, but people cannot tell who is the father and who is the son!" God caused a miracle and made Abraham appear much older (Baba Metzia 87a). Abraham thanked God for that miracle. After all, an older body was a sign of wisdom and of life experience.

How opposite this rabbinic midrash seems from the contemporary attitude that worships youth. Even if we care for our bodies, eat well, exercise and get enough sleep, our bodies grow older. The Torah teaches that one should "Rise before the hoary head" (Leviticus 19:32). An older body deserves respect, if just for the fact that it has survived. Usually it contains a soul that has accumulated wisdom through years of living.

The Spaniards searched for the Fountain of Youth and failed in their quest. Today, we seek a contemporary fountain of youth, trying to put off the inevitable with plastic surgery. Certainly, cosmetic surgery may have a role in helping someone cope with psychological problems or low self-esteem, but there is value in accepting that our bodies wear down over time.

In a wonderful scene in the movie *City Slickers*, Billy Crystal looks in the mirror at his forty-something body and remarks, "This is the best I am going to look for the rest of my life." If we see the world in purely material terms, aging is depressing. Material things wear down over time.

However, if we view the world in spiritual terms, we

recognize that we grow over time. We read more books, travel to more places, meet more people, do more good deeds and accumulate more of life's experiences. We can grow our souls. I recently turned fifty, and I know my body is not what it was at twenty-five. Yet, the Talmud teaches that fifty is the "age of advice" (Avot 5:21). Now I realize that I have lived long enough and grown my soul enough that I am ready to give advice to others.

Many of us seek perfect bodies. Men want to look like star athletes; women want to look like supermodels. How many teenage girls starve themselves? Or eat and binge to maintain the unnatural women's figures depicted in magazines? How many teenage boys experiment with steroids and other harmful chemicals to look like athletes? In real life, how many of us look like movie stars, supermodels or superathletes?

There is a blessing formulated by the rabbis upon seeing someone who looks different or unusual. "Praised art Thou, Lord our God, King of the Universe, Who varies His creation." The blessing indicates that God makes us in all shapes and sizes, with all kind of bodies. I can testify after performing hundreds of weddings that people with all kinds of bodies are able to find and share true love.

People of all shapes and sizes can be sexually attractive.

The Talmud tells this story:

> *A rabbi came across an extremely ugly man. The rabbi said, "Are all the people of your town as ugly as you?" The man answered, "Go tell the Workman how ugly is the vessel He created." Suddenly the rabbi felt terrible and begged the man for forgiveness* (Taanit 20a–b).

God created a variety of bodies, and none are perfect in the way we define perfection. In fact, a fascinating piece of rabbinic wisdom in the Talmud says that a married couple ought to enjoy sexual relations with the lights out. In the dark, they will not see each other's blemishes and physical imperfections (Niddah 17a). Few of us marry people who have bodies like the celebrities we admire. (In fact, many celebrities do not have the bodies we think they have. Plastic surgery, stand-in models, airbrushing and trick photography create the looks we admire.)

Our bodies may not meet our personal expectations, but they are God's gift to us. They belong to God, and we are the temporary occupants. Treating our bodies with respect is, therefore, more than a good health measure; it is a religious act.

Why the Body?

If our bodies are fragile, if they eventually die, if they need such care, why do we need them anyway? Perhaps we would be better off if we ignored our bodies and simply concentrated on matters of the spirit. Perhaps we should see our bodies as marred, imperfect vehicles preventing our souls from pursuing their destinies.

Under the influence of Plato, Greek philosophy tended to downplay the physical, material world in favor of a more spiritual world. The material world is changeable, the Greeks observed, and therefore imperfect. Plato compared the experience of the material world to living in a cave and looking at shadows reflected on a wall. In this world one sees only the reflections of the perfect spiritual world that is outside.

Plato had a huge influence on the Gnostics and other sects who tended to downplay the body and the material world and advised people to try to escape the world of the physical for a purer spiritual world. This philosophy is also hugely influential among Eastern mystics. In the godly life, those mystics say, one escapes the limitations of the body and the material world in order to connect with the pure spiritual world.

The biblical vision is very different. *The spirit needs the body.* The soul takes on a bodily existence in order to fulfill its particular mission on this earth. Of course the body dies, and the soul returns to God, Who gave it. But while on this earth, the soul must have a body to accomplish its God-given tasks. Both Jews and Christians pray that someday the soul will be rejoined with the resurrected body.

This joining of body and soul is reflected in the Talmudic story about sin and punishment:

> *The body is called before the highest court for the sins it committed on the earth. It replies, "Don't blame me. It is the soul's fault. Without the soul, I would merely lie here dead." The soul is then called before the highest court for the sins it committed on the earth. It replies, "Don't blame me. It is the body's fault. Without the body, I would be a mere ghost,*

unable to function in the physical world."

The judge then calls them both together. He says, "This reminds me of a blind man and a lame man accused of stealing figs from an orchard. The blind man claims, 'Don't blame me. I cannot see the fruit.' The lame man claims, 'Don't blame me. I cannot walk into the orchard.' Each alone may be innocent. But together, the lame man can climb on the blind man's shoulders and act as his eyes and hands, while the blind man acts as his legs. Together they are guilty."

The judge continues, "So, too, the soul and the body together would be guilty" (Sanhedrin 91a–b).

If the sins we commit on this earth need a body and soul working together, how much more so is that true of our good deeds. The body needs the soul and the soul needs the body. Without a body, the soul cannot accomplish its mission. "The dead cannot praise God" (Psalms 115:17). Without a soul, the body becomes mere inert matter. With the eternal joined to the temporal, humans do both good and wicked deeds. We fulfill our eternal destiny in a material world.

Guideposts for Your Fifth Journey: From Frailty to Health

1. Begin each morning with a blessing of thanks for the miracle of your body. You can use the blessing from the beginning of this chapter. Or write your own. Thank God that you are able to sleep and awaken again each day.

2. Do a physical self-assessment. What are your own physical strengths, and what are your shortcomings? Begin with a thorough examination by a physician. Are there chronic diseases that prevent your body from functioning at maximum efficiency? How is your weight? Do you get enough sleep? Do you exercise? What is your stress level? Do you have bad habits such as smoking or drinking? What can you do to improve your physical self?

3. Learn to read your own body. I recall a time when I consulted with a nutritionist because my eating was out of control. She told me how my mind was attuned to my body's needs. Before I eat, she told me, I should record in a notebook how hungry I am and what food I truly desire. After I eat, I should record how full I am. How does my body

feel after eating particular foods? I found her advice extremely helpful not only in gaining some self-control, but also in appreciating the miracle of my own body.

4. God has given your mind the ability to read your body's inner needs. You know when you are hungry, and if you carefully look inward, you can usually discern what kind of food your body desires. You can tell what foods make you feel good and which do not. You know when you lack sleep, and you know how many hours of sleep help you function at peak efficiency. You can usually tell when you are stressed and need a rest. Remember the sacred cycle of work and rest we humans desperately need (see chapter 4).

5. If you are stricken with a disease, use it as an opportunity to seriously assess your lifestyle. One can speculate how often chronic diseases occur because they are the only way our bodies can tell us we need to stop some behavior. How often have I visited someone in the hospital after a heart attack and heard them say, "My body was telling me it's time to slow down. But I didn't listen."

6. Take time to pamper your body. Get a massage, facial, manicure, pedicure, herbal treatment, visit a spa or sit in a whirlpool. Take time to shop leisurely for attractive clothing. Learn from the great sage Hillel, who took time out of his teachings to go to the bathhouse.

7. Learn to ignore physical imperfections. They too are a gift from God. No one, not even a super-model or superathlete, is born with a perfect body.

8. If you are lucky and live long enough, your body will grow older. You can view aging as a physical breaking down, or you can see aging as a time of spiritual growth. Elders are a source of wisdom. Learn to keep the Torah's commandment to respect elders. This includes respecting your own self as you grow older. Rabbi Zalman Schachter gives seminars called "Eldering" that focus on how to use the senior years to become mentors to the world.

The Creator of Our Bodies

The Torah teaches that God formed humans out of the dust of the earth. If we see our bodies as belonging to God, it helps us develop a deep sense of gratitude for our physical existence on this earth. As Jews throughout the world pray on Yom Kippur evening, "As clay we are, as soft and yielding clay, that lies between the fingers of the potter." From a simple law of torts, we learn the profound religious ideal that

God is our Creator.

6

Adversity

The Journey from Pain to Healing

Abram said, "O Lord God, what can You give me, seeing that I shall die childless?"

Genesis 15:2

When Rabbi Yohanan fell ill, Rabbi Hanina went to visit him and asked, "Are your sufferings welcome to you?" Rabbi Yohanan replied, "Neither them nor their reward." Rabbi Hanina said, "Give me your hand." Rabbi Yohanan gave him his hand and Rabbi Hanina raised him up from his sickbed.

Berachot 5b

The cantor of my congregation, Grigory Groysman, tells the following story. He learned it from his grandfather in Odessa, Ukraine, and it gave him comfort during years of suffering as a refusenik in the former Soviet Union:

A little boy befriended an old man. Every day the boy would go over to speak with the man and listen to his stories. The man had lived a very difficult life, with much pain and suffering. He was stooped over and scarred. He shared with the boy his sufferings and showed him his many scars. The boy felt sorry for the old man.

One day, on the way to the old man's house, the boy found a bird with a broken wing. He took the bird home, taped up its wing and told the bird he would help him heal. The bird was a magical bird, and he thanked the boy. The bird told the boy that he had the power to take away pain and suffering, to erase the scars, to make someone young and hopeful once again. The boy was thrilled and ran with the bird to the old man's house.

"This is a magical bird. He can take away all of your scars and make your pain go away. He can take

*away your suffering and make you young again. I
am so happy."*

*The old man looked at the little boy and the bird
with the taped-up wing. "My son, that is so kind of
you. Certainly nobody likes suffering nor pain. But
my suffering has made me into who I am. To erase
my pain is to erase part of me. No, thank you. I
would rather live with my suffering and my scars."*

Abraham and Sarah had their share of pain and suffering. In particular, they were childless. God promised
Abraham that his seed would be as uncountable as the
stars in the sky; yet he and his wife had reached old age
without ever having a child. At one point Abraham
cried out to God about the pain he felt that he might die
childless (Genesis 15:2).

Abraham and Sarah were not entirely passive about
their pain. They took action. Sarah asked Abraham to
participate in a surrogate-mother situation by having a
baby with her handmaiden Hagar. Sarah thought that
her lineage would be built through Hagar. Abraham did
have a baby with Hagar, a boy named Ishmael. Unfortunately, there was conflict between Sarah and

Hagar, and eventually Abraham had to drive both Hagar and Ishmael out of his home.

Then Abraham prayed for the pagan king Abimelech when the wombs of the women of Abimelech's kingdom closed up. In the very next biblical scene, God blessed Abraham and Sarah with a baby. The rabbis suggest that by praying for someone else facing the same crisis, Abraham and Sarah found their own cure (Baba Kama 92a). Thus, this story provides a fascinating insight about how to deal with loss: Facing adversity begins with helping others.

The sixth journey of life is the journey through adversity, going from pain to healing. Nobody escapes this journey. We each must know some pain in our lives, and the longer we live, the more pain we suffer. Pain and suffering are inevitable in this material world, as the following classic story relates.

A woman in great pain goes to her rabbi for solace. The rabbi tells her, "I want you to bake a loaf of bread. But I want you to bake it from flour that you borrow from others. One more rule: You can only borrow the flour from households that have never known pain and unhappiness."

The woman heeds the rabbi's advice and searches from household to household for a cup of flour. There is no one who has not known pain and suffering. Finally, the woman returns to the rabbi. "I realize I am not alone in my suffering."

Coping with Adversity

There is no life that does not contain some pain. Nobody totally escapes loss. As the Bible puts it, "There was no house where there was not someone dead" (Exodus 12:30). Death may take many forms. It may be an actual death of a loved one, or it may be the death of a dream, the death of hope.

The Talmud teaches that to be unable to conceive a child is a kind of a death (Nedarim 64b), and Abraham and Sarah coped with infertility. Illness also can be a kind of death: the death of the illusion that we are invulnerable.

My own rabbinic experience has taught me that many losses are a kind of death. I have counseled people coping with grievous losses: divorce, illness, bankruptcy, family estrangement, the loss of dreams. The mourning symptoms for all of these losses can be the same as when a loved one dies: shock, anger, guilt, depression, loss of faith, loneliness. Unlike an actual death, no traditional rituals are available to help people cope with such losses. Often they feel alone, abandoned by God in an indifferent universe. Sometimes they feel cursed by God or believe that they have sinned and received God's punishment.

This chapter explores the journey toward healing and wholeness. The losses are real, but humans have a God-given ability to cope with their losses, to continue to function and to move beyond the loss. The pain may not go away totally. But our losses become part of our being, they make us the people we are. The scars hurt, sometimes deeply, but they also help form us. As the philosopher Friedrich Wilhelm Nietzsche taught, "What doesn't kill me makes me stronger."

A path to healing is available even when we are in pain. A vital point about this healing journey is that *there is a difference between healing and a cure.* A cure makes a loss go away completely. Some diseases can be cured, but many cannot. Some losses disappear, while others stay with us throughout our earthly existence. Healing is the ability to live with our losses, to find wholeness, faith and a sense of purpose in spite of our losses. Healing can occur even when there is no cure. We can be at one with the universe, with God and with ourselves even after coping with death. I have watched many people again experience joy, even after grievous losses.

Five vital activities lead from pain to healing, five guideposts I use in helping people cope with adversity. They are action, time, people, good deeds and faith. Let us explore each one.

Action as Healer

I once met a deeply religious Christian couple suffering because of infertility. Having dealt with infertility in my own marriage, I spoke with the couple about whether to pursue aggressive medical treatment. They told me, "Rabbi, we realize that if God wanted us to have a baby, we would have one. This is obviously God's will for us. We must accept His decision." They seemed totally at peace, accepting with faith their circumstances. I almost envied their serenity.

I admire their calm acceptance and passivity in the face of adversity, but it is not the approach of most of the people I counsel. Nor was it the approach of Abraham and Sarah. They fought against their infertility with every weapon available in their time. They prayed and cried out to God. They tried using a surrogate mother. They tried adoption when Abraham said his servant Eliezer would become his heir. To Abraham and his family, passivity in the face of adversity was not a virtue. Action is the touchstone of the biblical approach.

A similar lesson can be seen in the story of the crossing of the Red Sea. The Israelites, fleeing Egypt, were trapped. The sea stood before them, the pursuing Egyptian army was behind them. Moses stood and prayed, until God finally said, "Why do you cry out to Me? Tell the Israelites to go forward" (Exodus 14:15). According to a classic rabbinic midrash, one of the princes of the people, Nachshon, the son of Aminadav, plunged into the sea. When the water was up to his neck, the sea parted. The Israelites were able to go forward to safety (Mechilta BeShalach 5).

This story is a cry for action in the face of adversity. Pushing forward, researching the problem, finding experts and doing are often the beginning of healing. I have counseled many people coping with difficult illness. The first step after the shock wears off is for them to become experts on their own medical conditions. I have seen people read books and articles, comb the Internet, contact research hospitals and medical experts, and seek alternative cures. Often the activity energizes them.

Like Nachshon, when adversity hits we need to plunge forward into the sea. We need to struggle with God, not simply accept our fate. That is certainly what my wife and I did when we learned that we were infertile. There was no time to bemoan our situation. I remember waking up from an unsuccessful surgery to correct an infertility problem and hearing my doctor ask, "Rabbi, do you want to impregnate your wife? Or do you want to be a father, even if the sperm comes from someone else?" We decided that we would do anything, as long as it was legal and moral, to become parents. We sought the best medical advice, including some unconventional techniques. Eventually, we turned to adoption, actively searching out adoptive situations. That is how we found our three children.

I see countless other examples in my day-to-day counseling of people who react to adversity with action. I think of the rabbi who was fired from a synagogue after many years serving his community. After an initial bout of depression, he started a successful and fulfilling business. Today he blesses the synagogue board that fired him. I think of the woman abandoned by her husband with two small children. She had never dreamed she would become a divorcée and single mom. Today she runs an active singles group and has a wonderful social life.

If God sent this adversity our way, we may wonder, why should we not passively accept it as God's will? The answer is that the Bible does not advocate passivity. When God finished creating the world, He looked at it and said it is "very good" (Genesis 1:31). Very good perhaps, but not yet perfect. Our job as humans is to perfect the world. The biblical creation story is really a call for action.

Of course, action is not always successful or even possible. There are times when we suffer losses for which there is no action, such as the death of a loved one.

There are times when we hear our doctors say, "There is no more that we can do." At these times, perhaps the best approach is Reinhold Niebuhr's popular recovery prayer:

Lord, give me the courage to change the things I can, the serenity to accept the things I cannot change and the wisdom to know the difference.

When we have done all we can do and there is no more action we can take, how do we find serenity? It begins with the realization that healing is not instantaneous; it takes time.

Time as Healer

I counsel people who have suffered grievous losses. Often they wonder how they will ever cope, become whole and find healing. I see them a year or two later and they have begun to enjoy life again. The wound may still be there, but time has ameliorated the hurt.

Holocaust survivors in my congregation have lost their entire families, everyone they knew, at the hands of the Nazis. They suffered horribly in the camps. Yet somehow, they have rebuilt their lives, established new families, found faith and learned to live lives of relative normalcy. In speaking with these survivors, I realize that their pain never goes away completely. Still, time becomes a healer.

The Bible, in one of its most famous passages, teaches:

To every thing there is a season, and a time for every purpose under heaven.

A time to be born and a time to die.

A time for planting and a time for uprooting.

A time for slaying and a time for healing.

A time for tearing down and a time for building up.

A time for weeping and a time for laughing.

A time for wailing and a time for dancing
(Ecclesiastes 3:1–4).

Time is a healer. Jewish tradition recognizes this when it teaches how to cope with the death of a loved one: *shiva*—seven days of intense mourning at home; *shloshim*—thirty days of less intense mourning during which celebrations are avoided; *avel*—a year of mourning during which memorial prayers are said each morning and evening. After a year, the mourning period ends. The mourner must reenter the world and begin participating again. When people are unable after a year to cope with their losses, I advise them to seek professional counseling.

A time of mourning is useful for all kinds of adversity, all the deaths that life throws our way. As King David wrote in his most famous psalm, "Though I walk through the valley of the shadow of death, I fear no harm for You are with me" (Psalms 23:4). We must walk through the valley, a journey that takes time but that eventually we complete. We need not dwell in the valley of the shadow of death forever. Time diminishes the pain.

Like the old man in the cantor's story, with time we integrate the pain into our beings. It becomes part of who we are. We are rebuilt into someone stronger. So often people ask me, "Rabbi, will the pain ever go away?" I answer, "No, it will never completely disappear. But it will diminish with time."

People as Healer

In the Bible story, Job suffered the most grievous losses anyone can know. He lost his children, he lost his wealth, he lost his health. His three friends—Eliphaz, Bildad and Zophar—came to visit him and simply sat next to him while waiting for him to speak. Their presence was a source of comfort. From this story, the rabbis derived the law that when visiting a mourner one should simply sit next to them and let the mourner speak first.

When we suffer adversity, we need the presence of other people. We need to speak to them. Talking is often the first step toward healing, which is why I tell grieving people to find a counselor or join a support group.

Any clergy member can relate to the following experience: Someone is going through pain in their life. He or she sets up an appointment and comes by to speak. The rabbi, priest or minister listens sympathetically, nodding affirmatively and offering little advice. When the session is over, the congregant thanks the clergy member profusely and says, "You were so helpful," when actually he or she did nothing but listen. The very act of talking removes some of the pain.

Rabbinic tradition recognizes this fact. It made it a *mitzvah* (good deed) to visit the sick. According to a rabbinic source, each visitor takes away one sixtieth of illness and suffering (Nedarim 39b). Other people can be healers.

Unfortunately, adversity too often becomes an excuse to turn inward and avoid others. People feel that they are alone in their suffering. Sometimes, longtime members of my synagogue will drift away when facing crises in their lives. The man facing bankruptcy, the woman smitten with breast cancer or the couple facing divorce will quietly disappear from the synagogue pew. When people most need a church, a synagogue or a community, they will stay away. Sometimes they are embarrassed. Sometimes they do not want to be a burden. Sometimes they want to be left alone in their pain.

I tell people that the synagogue, the community, consists of people who are there to help them face difficult times. Members of a house of worship often will pray for a person who is suffering. There seems to be some evidence, even if only anecdotal, that such prayers by the community are effective. Perhaps it is psychological, perhaps there is a mystical power to such prayers. Regardless, when facing adversity, people can be healers.

Good Deeds as Healer

Abraham prayed for King Abimelech and the women in his kingdom because God had closed up the women's wombs. After Abraham's prayer, God remembered Sarah, and Abraham and Sarah finally had a baby of their own. Isaac, the son of their old age, was born.

The rabbis teach that when Abraham prayed for someone else, God answered Abraham's own prayer. Sometimes when we are in pain or facing adversity, the best thing we can do is help others facing the same pain. In helping others, we soon find a sense of meaning and purpose to our own suffering. Giving to those in need diminishes our own pain.

One of the most powerful healers is a support group. Such groups exist for coping with every kind of adversity under the sun: loss of a parent or spouse, loss of a child, divorce, every kind of chronic illness, infertility, financial disappointment and various kinds of addictions. Invariably, grief support groups are led by other people who have suffered the same loss, often several years earlier, and have found healing by helping others facing the identical loss.

Those facing adversity can find healing in other ways. I have spoken to many older people in my community who have lost their spouses. They are often lonely and paralyzed, unable to take action to refocus their lives. I always advise volunteer work. Going to a local hospital, school, synagogue or church, charity organization and doing for others—through these, one begins to feel a renewed sense of purpose in life. It is true that cancer survivors raise the most money for cancer research, just as people who turn to a synagogue in time of need often take a leadership role within that synagogue. Adversity stimulates good deeds. Good deeds are healers.

Sometimes adversity can be the incentive behind projects to improve the world rather than wallow in self-pity. One woman who lost her young daughter to a drunk driver formed an organization named MADD— Mothers Against Drunk Driving. Her organization, more than any other initiative, has helped to stigmatize drunk drivers and cut back on the number of fatalities.

Though time is a healer, there comes a time when we need to stop dwelling in our own self-pity. The best way to move forward is to take on a project to improve the lives of others. To cope with my grief, I chose to write a book about infertility and adoption, a book that has allowed me to counsel countless couples coping with infertility. In doing for others, I get to see those who suffer begin to laugh, smile and live once again. Good deeds become the healer.

Faith as Healer

I was feeling very depressed one day as I drove along in my car. Things were not going my way at the synagogue. I flipped through the radio stations, trying to find something that would lift me up and refresh my spirit. I came across a country station, a form of music I rarely listen to. The station was playing Kenny Rogers's classic hit *The Gambler,* whose lyrics tell about knowing when to hold 'em and when to fold 'em. As I listened to the song, one of the lyrics jumped out at me. It spoke of poker hands and how every hand's a winner and every hand's a loser. What a profound insight about life that I needed to hear at that particular moment.

In life we have to play the hand we are dealt. Every hand has the potential of being a loser; every life situation can lead to depression, emptiness and a profound sense that life is meaningless. At the same time, every hand has the potential of being a winner; every life situation can lead to healing, optimism and a profound sense of purpose.

We can look at the universe and see a place of meaning and joy, a place where our prayers are answered and our lives have meaning. Or we can look at the same universe and see a place of emptiness, a dark cosmos indifferent to human suffering. It all depends on our perception.

A man comes to a new city and sees a woman sitting by the gate. "What are the people like in this city?" he asks. The woman responds, "What were the people like in the city you came from?" The man scoffs, "They were all crooks. They would steal the shirt off your back." The woman answers, "They are that way here, also."

A second man comes to the new city and sees the woman sitting by the gate. "What are the people like in this city?" The woman responds, "What were people like in the city you came from?" The man says, "They were wonderful. They would give you the shirt off your back." "They are that way here, also."

Attitude makes all the difference. I remember speaking to a very Orthodox man who had just been through some profound suffering. His marriage had broken up and he no longer had access to his children. I commented, "You must feel very much alone." He looked at me calmly and said, "I am never alone. God is always with me." I cannot say that I always share his faith, but I do believe that such faith is the ultimate source of healing.

A similar idea was presented by psychologist and Holocaust survivor Victor Frankl in his book *Man's Search for Meaning.* He lost most of his family and suffered horribly under the Nazis. He realized that ultimately we have no control over external factors and what the world sends our way. The only thing we can control is our attitude toward it. Frankl believes that we humans can survive anything if only we can find meaning in our experience.

It is possible to see a universe where God is there for us, where God helps us through difficult and painful times. Sometimes it is useful to remember the classic story of the footprints on the sand.

A man looked back on his life and saw two sets of footprints in the sand. He realized that one set was

his own and one set was God's. However, as he con-
tinued to look back, he saw the most difficult,
painful moments of his life. During these times he
saw only one set of footprints. Feeling abandoned,
the man cried out to God, "There is only one set of
footprints during the hard times. Where were you,
God?" And the voice of God answered, "Those were
the times I carried you!"

The Book of Psalms teaches that "God is the healer of broken hearts" (Psalms 147:3). The belief that life has a purpose can give us the power to find meaning when the world looks bleak and hopeless. We are not in this world by chance; God placed us here. Perhaps we cannot always comprehend why things happen, but faith is a healer.

Guideposts for Your Sixth Journey: From Pain to Healing

1. Tell yourself that suffering is not a punishment from God. We do not live in a universe of simplistic reward and punishment. There is no reason to add guilt to the pain of suffering by feeling that we suffer because of our sins. Adversity strikes

everyone, the good and the not-so-good alike. It comes as a result of living in a material universe.

2. One reason we face adversity is because we live in a world run by natural laws. In the Talmud, the rabbis ask why God allows stolen wheat to grow. Why does God not punish the thief by preventing the grain from sprouting? The answer is that the world behaves according to its nature (Avodah Zara 54b). Nature does not change her laws to reward the righteous or to punish the wicked. Perhaps if we lived a purely spiritual existence, we would know eternal bliss, but in a world of nature sometimes things go wrong.

3. When a crisis hits, do not make any rash decisions. While you're still in shock is not the time to quit your job, divorce your spouse, sell your home or take any other sudden, irreversible action. Sometimes change is a solution to crisis, but only after the passage of time. Such change should be undertaken only after careful introspection and with much forethought.

4. Remember that action is a healer. Consult with an objective observer to chart out a course of action.

Depending on the situation, such a person might be a physician, an attorney, a member of the clergy, a therapist, or a dear and trusted friend. The person must be both empathetic and somewhat dispassionate so that they can clearly discern options. It is difficult to decide on an intelligent course of action when emotions are churning.

5. Remember, time is a healer. Write the words "This Too Shall Pass" on a card and place it in your pocket. Look at the card whenever the emotions become overwhelming. A broken arm does not heal immediately, but with time it does heal. A broken heart may take even longer, but it also will heal.

6. Remember that people are healers. It is extremely tempting to isolate yourself when you are in pain. It is vital to seek people. Join a support group. Visit a therapist. Find a trusted family member or friend to talk to. Do not worry about being a burden. It may be a cliché, but it is still true that that's what friends are for.

7. Remember that good deeds are healers. Find a project that will make the world better. What can

you do to prevent someone else from suffering the pain you are suffering? Donate to a worthy cause. Write or speak publicly about your experience. (Today, numerous Holocaust survivors are sharing their stories with synagogues, churches and schools. Their words may help prevent a future Holocaust.) You are a survivor. Are you ready to share your experience with others?

8. Remember that faith is a healer. The next chapter speaks about the journey to spirituality. Perhaps this is the time to connect to your childhood faith. Begin attending a synagogue or church, or simply turn to God and pour out your heart.

Walk Through the Valley

The most popular of King David's 150 psalms is the twenty-third. It speaks of walking through the valley of the shadow of death, and each of us, as we go through life, must walk through that valley not once but several times. It is a painful walk, but one that makes us stronger. As Psalm 23 teaches, "I fear no evil, for you are with me. Your staff and your rod do comfort me" (Psalms 23:4). As we face the many deaths life sends our way, there is comfort and healing in knowing that

God is our Shepherd.

7

Spirituality

The Journey from Doubt to Faith

I will establish my covenant between Me and you, and I will make you exceedingly numerous.

Genesis 17:2

Therefore a person should say, the world was created for me.

Sanhedrin 4:5

A husband and wife went to a fine restaurant to celebrate their anniversary. The meal was delicious, and when it was over, the couple thanked the waiter profusely for bringing them such a delicious dinner.

The waiter replied, "Why do you thank me? I only brought you food that was prepared in our kitchen. Why don't you go back there and thank the chef?"

The couple went back to the kitchen to thank the chef for the meal, and he replied, "I appreciate your kind words, but why thank me? I simply combine and cook the many quality ingredients that our supplier brings me. Here is the company that supplies most of our products. Why don't you thank them?"

The couple went over to the supply company and thanked the truck driver. The truck driver replied, "Why thank me? I simply arrange transportation. It is the farmer who grows and produces the products that you eat. Why don't you thank the farmer?"

The couple drove out to the nearby farm and thanked the farmer for the many fresh products supplied. The farmer replied, "Why thank me? I plant the field and harvest the crops. I milk the cows and raise the chickens. But there is a force greater than me who supplies the food."

"Who is that?" The farmer looked up, and the couple understood to Whom they needed to give their thanks. They realized that the waiter, the chef, the supplier and the farmer are all partners, working with the Ultimate Provider. They turned their hearts and thanked God.

Finally, God made His covenant with Abraham. He promised that Abraham's children would be as uncountable as the stars in the sky, that through him would the nations of the world be blessed. Abraham promised that he would be ever faithful to the covenant. As a symbol of the covenant, God asked Abraham to circumcise himself and to circumcise on the eighth day every baby boy born into his family.

The creation of the covenant came rather late in the story of Abraham. Until that point, Abraham was not yet ready. He needed to leave and find his own identity, to learn self-control and delayed fulfillment. He needed to work on his family relationships and find a way to be a provider. He needed to worry about his physical being, and perhaps he needed to feel some pain in his life. (This reminds me of being told by an older woman, when I was a newly ordained rabbi, "You haven't suffered enough to be a rabbi yet." I hope I have suffered enough by now.)

Only then was Abraham ready for his true spiritual quest—just as we cannot begin our spiritual searching until other parts of our lives are in place. As a wise rabbi once said, "Without flour there can be no Torah" (Avot 3:21). Without having the physical parts of life in place, we cannot seek the spiritual parts.

According to a midrash, Abraham had sensed long before that there was a spiritual force at work in the universe. Even as a child he had seen the sun set when the moon came out, and the moon set when the sun came out. He knew that the ultimate force of the universe was greater than either the sun or the moon. He destroyed the idols in his father's shop because he knew that something made of wood and stone, something material, could not be the ultimate life force.

Tradition teaches that throughout his travels Abraham actively brought people to a belief in one God. According to Rashi's commentary, Abraham converted the men while Sarah converted the women. That is the meaning of the verse that says Abraham traveled with "the souls he made" (Genesis 12:5). How did Abraham succeed in these conversions? His tent was open on all sides, and every passerby was invited in to share a meal (Genesis Rabbah 48:9). When the meal was over, Abraham asked his guests to thank the One who provided the meal. Guests would first thank Abraham and Sarah, who replied that they were not the ultimate providers. Guests were eventually taught to say grace after meals, to thank God for their food (Genesis Rabbah 54:6). Tradition also teaches that Abraham invented daily prayer. He introduced the morning *(shacharit)* service, his son Isaac introduced the afternoon *(mincha)* service, and his grandson Jacob introduced the evening *(ma'ariv)* service (Berachot 26b). Three times a day, traditional Jews stop, turn their hearts toward heaven and pray.

The Spiritual Dimension

Some, including many scientists, would say that the physical, material dimension of life is all there is. To materialists, if something cannot be measured in a laboratory, it does not exist.

As Abraham knew, the human psyche has a deep yearning for something more, and something in the physical world seems to point to a spiritual force at work in the world. There is a spiritual dimension to existence. We may not be able to prove the existence of the spiritual; it may not be measurable in a laboratory. But it is present. In order to understand this spiritual force, we must first look at the material world. We must return to the laws of entropy presented in chapter 5.

What is entropy? Let us begin with these questions: Is the universe a perpetual-motion machine? Does it keep going and going, like the Energizer bunny? Or will the universe eventually wear down and grind to a halt? The answer lies in a scientific law discovered by nineteenth-century German scientist Rudolf Clausius: All systems eventually wear down. All things—rocks and mountains, humans, planets and suns, the universe itself—eventually wear down and die. The natural world is a dying world. The prophet Isaiah already said it thousands of years ago: "All the heavens shall wither like a leaf withering on the vine, or the shriveled fruit on a fig tree" (Isaiah 34:4). How does entropy work? If I hold my cold hand over a hot cup of coffee, my hand warms up and the coffee cools down. Eventually they will be the same temperature.

We can always make hot things hotter. That is how stoves work, but they require a huge influx of energy. We can always make cold things colder. That is how refrigerators work, but they also require a huge influx of energy. Without the influx of energy, all things wear down, fall apart and die. That is the way the universe works.

Rabbi Daniel Lapin of Seattle gives one of the best examples of entropy I have heard: Leave a brand-new car out in the woods for 200 years. After those years pass, a pile of rusted metal, paint, plastic and other materials remains. But if you leave rusted metal, paint and plastic in the woods for 200 years, they will never become a new car. Material things spontaneously fall apart; they do not spontaneously come together.

The universe, and everything in it, is dying. Entropy is increasing. Given enough time, energy will dissipate, matter will fall apart, all things will become more random and disorganized and the world will go back to the description in the first lines of Genesis: *tohu vavohu* — "void and without form." Entropy is an inexorable law of science, like gravity and the speed of light. The world of material things is a world that is dying. We live in an ever-dying universe, and because we are flesh and bones, we too must die.

But is there more? Is there anything that goes beyond the natural world? Is there a spiritual dimension? If there is such a force, it must be able to overcome entropy.

Let us look at another aspect of what science says about the universe: The universe started with a big bang. Cosmic dust exploded outward. Hydrogen atoms formed, and eventually these combined to make more complex atoms, including carbon. Carbon atoms joined together to make nuclei and proteins. Cells formed, first single-celled creatures, then more complex ones. Eventually, higher organisms formed, consciousness developed and these ultimately evolved into the highest form of all: human beings. This is the precise opposite of entropy! There is a force at work in the universe that seems to be directed toward the creation of life. According to every scientific law, it should never have happened. The universe should become more random, not more complex. If the material world is dying, the spiritual world is one that gives life.

The Bible contains a powerful metaphor that describes this life-sustaining force. The prophet Ezekiel saw a valley filled with bones, a valley of death, the natural result of entropy. God said to Ezekiel, "Son of man, can these bones live?" (Ezekiel 37:3). Ezekiel spoke to the bones, and they grew flesh and sinews. He spoke again, and a wind came "and the breath came into them, and they lived, and stood up upon their feet, an exceeding great host" (Ezekiel 37:10). This is anti-entropy at work, a spiritual force that overcomes death. I cannot prove that there is a God, but I see a universe teeming with life. And that points to a life-sustaining force beyond nature. If the physical universe is about death, the spiritual universe is about life.

How can we mortals relate to this spiritual dimension of existence? How can we tune in to the life-giving force of God? We know that the spiritual force is out there, even if we are not always aware of it.

Abraham's grandson Jacob had a dream of a ladder reaching to the heavens. Angels were climbing up and down the ladder. In the dream, God spoke to him and renewed His covenant with him. When Jacob awoke, he said, "Surely the Lord is present in this place, and I did not know it" (Genesis 28:16). He called the place Beth El, literally "House of God."

The spiritual force that sustains the universe is around us at all times. Spirituality is the ability to tune into that force, to sense its presence. One of the goals of religion is to develop methods of relating to the spiritual force. Various faith traditions contain various paths. Ultimately, their common goal is to find a way for us to say that "God is in this place and we knew it not" (Genesis 28:16).

Let us explore four different but congruent paths to spirituality. They are (1) cultivating deep gratitude, (2) spiritual disciplines, (3) acts of separation, and (4) acts of loving-kindness.

Cultivating Deep Gratitude

Over twenty years of service in the rabbinate have convinced me of a profound truth: *Spirituality begins with gratitude.* Abraham began his quest to bring people to one God by telling them to say grace after meals. Jewish tradition teaches that everyone should offer one hundred blessings of gratitude per day. We should each look at the universe and say, "Thank you."

Materialists see the universe as a cold, heartless place, indifferent to human beings and our dreams and desires. We exist by chance, the result of blind material forces. When we die we go into a black void. There is no room for gratitude in such a world view. The materialists would say that since the universe is apathetic to human needs and desires we ought to be indifferent to the universe.

Those who reject the materialist mindset see a universe that not only has permitted us to exist but allows us to succeed and flourish. Some scientists speak of the anthropic principle, which states that the universe is fine-tuned in such a way that humans can exist. For example, if gravity was a bit stronger, the stars would burn out without enough time for elements like carbon, the building block of life, to form and develop. If gravity was a bit weaker, the stars would become diffuse hydrogen gas, without the reactor power that energizes life. Scientists have noted that gravity, and other cosmological constants, are precisely set so that we humans can exist.

To the religious mind, not only does the universe

allow humanity as a whole to flourish but there is a force at work that has allowed each of us to be born and to exist. We were each chosen by God and given a mission on earth. Jews say a prayer each morning when they arise: "I thank you, living Sovereign of the Universe, for returning my soul to me in kindness. How great is Your faithfulness." As I said in chapter 1, there are three partners in the creation of every human being: a mother, a father and God.

Spirituality begins for each of us when we say "thank you" to the universe. As the Talmud teaches, it begins by our saying, "The world was created for me" (Sanhedrin 4:5). It begins by seeing the universe not as a cold, indifferent place but as a place fine-tuned for each of us to exist and flourish. Saying "thank you" develops the mindset of inner peace, appreciation and gratitude necessary for a spiritual life.

Spiritual Disciplines

Every religious faith develops certain spiritual disciplines, such as prayer, ritual, meditation, song or dance.

The purpose of all spiritual disciplines is to provide an opportunity to stop life's routines to better tune in to the spiritual dimension.

The key is discipline. There is no such thing as instant spirituality. The story in chapter 2 of the woman who called me after Yom Kippur illustrates this point well. The woman had come to my congregation's services for the first time, having not set foot in a synagogue for many years. She sat for half an hour and then left. And she complained to me, "Rabbi, I waited a half hour for something spiritual to happen, but nothing happened."

God stands outside of time. Only with the creation of the universe was time itself formed. We humans need to cultivate moments when we also exist outside time. Religion teaches the centrality of regular prayer, regular rituals and regular moments of meditation because such actions lift us above the mundane and allow us to tune in to the spiritual dimension, to attain a certain timelessness in such moments. When we can touch eternity, we can begin to sense God's presence.

In my own tradition, this sense of eternity is achieved through regular daily prayer. I pray three times a day, and I am well aware of criticisms of Jewish prayer. It is said that Jewish prayers move too fast, they are in Hebrew, no one understands them, participants spend more time talking to each other than to God, and the services are sexist and have traditionally excluded women. There is truth in each of these criticisms.

Nonetheless, I have found a true spiritual benefit to this daily practice. First, the very quickly spoken Hebrew words turn into a kind of mantra. Even those who do not know Hebrew can achieve a mental state beyond the here and now. Also, the words are very ancient, some of them more than three thousand years old. When we consider that the same words are being used all over the world, and have been for centuries, we discover timelessness in the prayer services. Often I feel like I am part of something greater than myself.

People have asked me if I always feel this sense of spirituality when I participate in Jewish prayer? No, I don't. Sometimes my prayers are just routine. But then, I do not always feel great joy when I participate in my three-times-per-week exercise routine. Like exercise, the value of prayer is sometimes in the day-in, day-out dis-cipline of doing it. Now and again, as I pray, the here and now fades, and I feel myself part of something very deep and very ancient. I stand outside of time and I feel connected to the spiritual source of the universe. I find myself saying, as Jacob said after his dream, God is in this place and I knew it not.

Other religious traditions have their own spiritual disciplines. Christians stop for a moment of grace before eating a meal, connecting the physical to the spiritual. Church rituals, whether the classic Catholic mass or Protestant hymns, create in the worshiper a sense of timelessness. In the Buddhist tradition, daily meditation allows believers to remove themselves from the physical world and connect to the spiritual dimension. Discipline is vital to spirituality in all faiths.

Acts of Separation

The Torah teaches, "You shall be holy for I the Lord God am holy" (Leviticus 19:2). The biblical commentator Rashi teaches that the word "holiness" means separated. God created the universe through acts of separation. In the first chapter of Genesis, God separated darkness from light, the upper waters from the lower waters, the water from the dry land, the kingdom of plants from the kingdom of animals. One of the key ideas of numerous religions is *imitatio deo,* the imitation of God. We achieve holiness through our acts of separation and distinction.

Perhaps the most important act of separation is to designate one day in seven as the Sabbath, the day of rest. Jewish women often come to me on a spiritual quest, asking how to bring God into their lives. My first piece of advice has always been to light Shabbat candles on Friday before sundown. That is the first step toward holiness.

Wayne Muller, a Christian pastor, has written a beautiful book about the spiritual discipline of the Sabbath. In it, he writes:

> *All life requires a rhythm of rest. There is a rhythm in our waking activity and the body's need for sleep. There is a rhythm in the way day dissolves into night, and night into morning. There is a rhythm as the active growth of spring and summer is quieted by the necessary dormancy of fall and winter. There is a tidal rhythm, a deep, eternal conversation between the land and the great sea. In our bodies, the heart perceptibly rests after each life-giving beat; the lungs*

rest between the exhale and the inhale.

We have lost this essential rhythm. Our culture invariably supposes that action and accomplishment are better than rest, that doing something— anything—is better than doing nothing. Because of our desire to succeed, to meet these ever-growing expectations, we do not rest. Because we do not rest, we lose our way (Muller, 1999, p. 1).

Beginning each Friday night as the sun is setting, my family stops its regular routine. My wife lights candles and I bless each of my children, then we say the traditional prayers over wine and challah. My children know that malls and movies, sporting events and parties are off-limits to us at that time. They do not always love it, but it does add a sense of godliness to their lives.

Religious Christians and Muslims observe Sabbaths on Sunday and Friday, respectively. The details of individual observance may vary, but the notion of separation from the weekday world remains vital.

The purpose of the Sabbath is to force us to stop and reflect. If life is a series of journeys, on a regular basis we must stop, take our bearings, read the compass, take a breath and consider our path.

Other acts of separation and holiness are part of the daily spiritual practices of Judaism. For example, Jews separate the animal kingdom into animals permitted for food and those prohibited. Even among permitted animals, one may not eat the meat of the animal together with its milk. This symbolizes a separation of life and death; milk is the life-giving force of animals, flesh is obtained through the death of the animal.

Some other faith communities have similar practices of separation and holiness, including various dietary laws. Muslims avoid pork and abstain from alcohol. Catholics mark the period of Lent by abstaining from certain foods and other pleasures. By imitating God's acts of separation during the creation, we humans can add a spiritual dimension to our own lives.

Acts of Loving-Kindness

I once knew a man who decided to live by himself in a cabin in the woods, minimizing contact with others while seeking communion with God. I remember questioning him, "Can you connect with God while being disconnected from humanity?" One of the great truths of our various religious traditions is that the spiritual dimension is found in the midst of humanity.

Until now, each of the paths to spirituality I have mentioned can be done by individuals themselves, rather than as part of a community. One of the greatest criticisms I have of the contemporary quest for spirituality is that it often becomes privatized and disconnected from others. Yet one can connect to God as easily in their community as on a mountaintop.

Spirituality through connection with others is reflected in one of the most beautiful passages in all of rabbinic literature, a passage about the true meaning of imitating God (Sotah 14a):

Rav Hama, son of Rav Hanina, said, "What is the meaning of the verse 'Follow none but the Lord your God'" (Deuteronomy 13:15)? Is it possible for a human being actually to follow the ways of God? Has it not already been said, "The Lord your God is a devouring fire" (Deuteronomy 4:24)? What it means is that we should imitate the attributes of God.

As God clothed the naked, as it is written, "And

the Lord God made for Adam and his wife garments of skin and He clothed them" (Genesis 3:21), so you should clothe the naked.

As God visited the sick, as it is written, "The Lord appeared to Abraham by the terebinths of Mamre" (Genesis 18:1, after Abraham's circumcision), so you should visit the sick.

As God comforted mourners, as it is written, "After the death of Abraham, God blessed his son Isaac" (Genesis 25:11), so you should comfort mourners.

As God buried the dead, as it is written, "He buried him [Moses] in the valley" (Deuteronomy 34:6), so also you should bury the dead.

God is found within community. In the next chapter, I explore the journey from self to community. Part of the wisdom of many inherited spiritual traditions is that among our fellow human beings we find a sense of ultimate purpose and belonging. Perhaps the philosopher Martin Buber put it best when he wrote about I-Thou relationships.

I-Thou is a total relationship between two human beings. It is nonutilitarian, mutually beneficial, almost timeless. An I-Thou relationship has a spiritual dimension. To Buber, it is only in such relationships that we come to know God. "Every particular Thou is a glimpse through to the Eternal Thou." Such relationships lift our lives above a mundane, animal existence and allow us to be attuned to our Creator.

Guideposts for Your Seventh Journey: From Doubt to Faith

1. Begin by cultivating in yourself a deep sense of gratitude. Even if you are not sure whether you believe in God, learn to say thank you to the universe. Say thank you that you are alive. Say thank you for the parts of your body that work properly. (Too often we only see the parts that do not work.) Say thank you for your family and friends. Say thank you for the food you eat, the clothing you wear and the roof over your head. Learn to show appreciation numerous times per day.

2. Doubt is natural, particularly in our skeptical day and age. Perhaps the best solution is to take a leap of action, to act as a believer. When the Israelites received the Torah, they said, "We will do and we

will understand" (Exodus 24:7). The action comes first, the understanding second. When we behave in a certain way, the heart usually follows.

3. If you have philosophical questions about God and faith, set up an appointment with your rabbi, priest or minister. Remember, they have also struggled with these same questions, often on a sophisticated level. Do not assume that religious faith is childish. On the contrary, the vast majority of the most highly respected philosophers in history wrote about their religious faith.

4. Begin to develop a spiritual discipline. It may be daily or weekly worship, meditation, or simply quiet prayer time. The key is discipline. Discipline must be exercised regularly, not simply when the mood hits. If you are of the Jewish faith, take a course in reading Hebrew and begin to find your way through the traditional Jewish prayer book.

5. Pick one day a week as your Sabbath. Learn the classical Sabbath observances of your faith or develop your own observances. What do you do to mark your Sabbath as holy and special? And what do you refrain from doing to set the day

apart? The Sabbath day of rest was considered so vital to the human psyche that God made "Remember the Sabbath and keep it holy" one of the Ten Commandments.

6. What other acts of separation and holiness can add spirituality to your life? Holiday observances? Dietary laws? Life-cycle events? Visiting holy places, making pilgrimages? Look for opportunities to infuse holiness into day-to-day living.

7. Find ways to practice acts of loving-kindness. Hug a child. Visit a shut-in. Bring flowers to a nursing home. Talk to someone feeling down. Read the next chapter for more ways to connect with community. Remember that every human being is created in the image of God.

Where Is God?

The Kotzker Rebbe once taught, "Where is God? Wherever we let God in." God exists outside of time and space. Every place and every time have the potential to become holy. Part of living is to find spiritual moments in every place and time in which we dwell.

Ultimately, we live in a universe created by God, infused with a spiritual force. The entire world has the potential to become a source of holiness. As the Book of Psalms so powerfully teaches us, "One thing I ask of the Lord, only that do I seek: to live in the house of the Lord all the days of my life, to gaze upon the beauty of the Lord and to dwell in His temple" (Psalms 27:4). The journey to spirituality allows us to look at the world and know that

God is our Dwelling Place.

8

Community

The Journey from Self to Others

Shall not the Judge of all the earth not do justly?

Genesis 18:25

If I am not for myself, who will be for me? But if I am only for myself, then what am I? If not now, when?

Hillel, Avot 1:14

Once upon a time there lived a king who ruled over a vast kingdom. His advisors wanted to find a bride for him. So they brought a woman, a princess, from a distant kingdom to meet the king.

Together the king and the princess sat on a couch. And the king began to talk. "I am master of this palace, with hundreds of servants in attendance, all who must answer me at my beck and call." And the woman moved away from him on the couch.

"I have an entire army of soldiers ready at my command to go into battle against our enemies." And the woman moved a little farther away.

"My kingdom is many square miles, with thousands of subjects who pay me taxes and must obey the rules and laws that I proclaim." And the princess moved even farther, to the other end of the couch.

"And I feel alone, and scared, and vulnerable and always pray that I am doing the right thing." Upon hearing this, the princess came closer, sat next to the king and took his hand.

In the previous chapter, I said that when we visit the sick we are imitating this act of kindness by God. We see this in the story of Abraham sitting in his tent while recovering from his circumcision. God came to visit him. Because his tent was open on all sides, it was easy for Abraham to see every passing caravan, every wanderer who might need some food to eat and a place to stay. Three messengers came by, and Abraham, though still recovering, rushed out to invite them in and to offer food. While guests in his tent, these messengers said that at this time next year Abraham's wife Sarah would give birth to a son. Sarah laughed, unable to believe that a son could be born to her in old age. Eventually, the son of Abraham and Sarah would be born and named Isaac, from the Hebrew root meaning "to laugh."

After the news of the forthcoming birth, the Bible presents one of its most powerful and dramatic scenes in the story of Sodom and Gemorrah. These cities had a scarcity complex and were unwilling to share their riches with the wayfarer and the poor, so God decided to destroy the two cities. Knowing that Abraham was a man of righteousness who would teach justice and charity to his children, God shared with him the plan to destroy the cities.

In a passionate argument, Abraham defended the

cities of Sodom and Gemorrah. "Perhaps fifty righteous people can be found there. Would You destroy the righteous with the wicked? Shall not the Judge of all the earth not do justly?" (Genesis 18:24–25). God said He would spare the cities for the sake of fifty righteous people. Abraham continued to argue. What if there are forty-five righteous people? Forty? Thirty? Twenty? Ten? Like a crafty shopper in the marketplace in Jerusalem, Abraham bargained with God. God agreed to save the cities even for ten righteous people. In the end, not even ten righteous people could be found. Only Abraham's nephew Lot and his family were allowed to flee. Fire and brimstone rained down. Lot's wife, looking back on family members left behind as the city was destroyed, was turned into a pillar of salt.

This great argument between Abraham and God is the story of a man willing to stand up for others, even for the strangers who lived in these wicked cities. It is perhaps the greatest example in the Bible of moving beyond one's self, of the importance of serving the community. As the great sage Hillel would later say, "Do not separate yourself from the community" (Avot 2:5).

Why Community?

At the dawn of creation, God said to the man He had made, "It is not good for man to be alone" (Genesis 2:18). Within the context of the Bible, this refers to marriage and family, but in a broader sense the verse could refer to the fundamental human need for others, for community.

We humans are social creatures. We give meaning to our lives through our relationships with other humans. In chapter 6, I noted how we can heal the pain of adversity by talking with others. The very act of sharing our pain with others is a fundamental step toward becoming whole again. Community gives us solace for our pain. It is also a source of pleasure, fellowship and sharing. At our most joyous times, our wedding and bar/bat mitzvah celebrations, our graduations and birthdays, we want to be with the people we care about. Life is to be lived in the midst of community.

Unfortunately, our modern Western culture, for all its comforts, is one of the loneliest in human history. Most of us are more disconnected than ever before. We leave the neighborhoods where we grew up to pursue careers around the country, even around the world. We live in fenced and gated communities. Most of us have never been in the homes of our neighbors; we may not even know their names.

More often than during any other time in history, we Americans are not joiners. Many of us belong to no church or synagogue, no organization, no PTA, not even a bowling league. (The title of a recent book on this subject by Robert Putnam says it all: *Bowling Alone*.) As a congregational rabbi, I find that many of my members pay dues to the synagogue but do not see themselves as part of a community. Too many see the synagogue as a service station, a place to meet their particular needs for a child's bar or bat mitzvah, a place to say the mourner's kaddish for parents, a place to pray on the High Holidays, a place to find a rabbi to meet spiritual needs. Most have not developed a sense of community, of truly living their lives among others.

Individualism is the hallmark of American culture, as Robert Bellah and his colleagues chronicled in their classic work *Habits of the Heart*: "American cultural traditions define personality, achievement and the purpose of human life in ways that leave the individual suspended in glorious, but terrifying, isolation" (p. 6). This individualism has certainly been one of the great gifts our culture gave the world. It is manifested in the great cultural myths of our tradition, from the lonely pioneers who left family to conquer the west to the Horatio Alger stories of individuals who pulled themselves out of difficult circumstances and succeeded in attaining their goals. Individualism teaches that we are not defined by tradition or community and that we need not conform to what others demand. We are free to form our own dreams and follow our own stars.

However, individualism also leads to a profound, existential loneliness. As the story at the beginning of this chapter about the king and the princess shows, we feel the need for others. We long for their voices and their touch. Human beings need to be connected to other human beings. The eighth great journey of life is the journey to community, the journey from self to others.

Why do we need others? The reason goes beyond our existential loneliness. Other humans make us better. When we hear on the news that a serial killer has been arrested, what word immediately jumps into our mind? Invariably, it's the word "loner." People who live disconnected from others are more likely to get into trouble, more likely to cause pain and more likely to lose their moral bearings.

We do not need to speak of serial killers to see this phenomenon. A person can work alone on a computer, undetected and disconnected, while designing and disseminating computer software viruses intended to harm individuals and society.

I regularly lead an online chat. People join my chat using screen names that mask their real identities. While they hide behind the anonymity of a screen name, I find that people behave much more crudely, with a much higher disregard for their fellow humans. I have witnessed behavior in these chat rooms that I would never see among people sitting in a room and speaking face to face.

We also see the effects of anonymity on the crowded streets of our highways. Aggressive driving, blaring music, road rage and antisocial behavior are created by the fact that people are hidden while in their cars. In a society where disconnectedness is common, antisocial behavior becomes rampant.

On the other hand, when we see our neighbors' faces, we are far more likely to feel their pain. We are less likely to hurt them. It is more likely that we will extend ourselves to help those whom we know, those who are members of our community. We need community to make us better.

Community is also important for another reason. Each of us has a mission, a purpose that we are trying to accomplish during our years on this earth. Our missions are not private matters that affect only ourselves. Ultimately, we carry out our missions in the midst of others, each carrying out our own particular task. Each of us carries a piece of a giant jigsaw puzzle, and removing our particular piece damages the whole picture.

This thought was probably best articulated by the Christian theologian Reinhold Niebuhr:

Nothing worth doing is completed in our lifetime; therefore we must be saved by hope.

Nothing true or beautiful or good makes complete sense in any immediate context of history; therefore we must be saved by faith.

Nothing we do, however virtuous, can be accomplished alone; therefore we are saved by love (Niebuhr, 1952).

Niebuhr's third statement is the essence of why we humans need community: Nothing worth doing can be accomplished alone. Great things happen when we join with others to complete a task.

There is a wonderful passage in the Talmud regarding Adam in the Garden of Eden: "Look how hard Adam had to work. If he wanted a meal he had to plant a seed, and then he had to harvest it, and then he had to winnow the chaff, and then he had to knead the dough and bake the bread. Whereas I can come to table and others have done all these things for me. . . . When Adam wanted to wear a garment, he had to cut the wool from the sheep, and then he had to wash it, and then he had to spin it and sew it. Whereas I go to the store, and all the work has been done for me by others" (Berachot 58a). Occasionally it is worth thinking of all the people who made us what we are: the parents who gave birth to us and raised us; the teachers who taught us; the coaches and youth leaders and rabbis, priests and ministers who led us and mentored us; the bosses who hired us and gave us opportunities; the families and friends who supported us; even the factory workers and farmers and storekeepers who provided for our needs.

Everything we are, everything we accomplish, even everything we consume is done in partnership with others. We cannot do it alone.

Community is the context for carrying out our mission. Each of us, wherever we live, must seek a community. Niebuhr taught that we are saved by love. Fundamental to life is the Golden Rule, expressed in the Bible by the powerful words "Love your neighbor as yourself" (Leviticus 19:18).

The Golden Rule

A non-Jew came to see the great sage Hillel. He said he wanted to convert to Judaism—but only if Hillel could tell him the entire Torah while standing on one foot. The non-Jew had already gone to Hillel's rival Shammai, who threw him out of his study. Now he challenged Hillel.

Hillel stood on one foot and said, "Whatever is hateful to you, do not do unto others. All the rest is commentary. Now, go and learn." The man converted (Shabbat 31a).

Hillel taught a passive formulation of the Golden Rule, a central tenet of every major faith throughout the world. Community begins with a basic respect for our fellow humans. To paraphrase the Hippocratic oath, Hillel instructed, "First, do no harm"—avoid any action that hurts or mars the image of God in any other human. The test of whether any action complies with this teaching is how we would feel if someone did it to us.

Countless laws in the Torah specify how to avoid hateful actions toward others. We are forbidden to steal, to cheat, to lie, to place a stumbling block before the blind, to curse the deaf, to have unfair weights and measures, to gossip, or to be a talebearer. All our actions ought to reflect the humanity and dignity of our fellow humans.

Sometimes I illustrate this interdependence of humanity with the image of a man sitting in a lifeboat who begins to drill a hole under his seat. The other passengers challenge him, but he insists, "It is my seat and I can do what I want with it." The passengers cannot convince him that they will all go down together if the boat floods. Each of our actions affects our fellow humans, sometimes in ways we cannot immediately comprehend.

The Golden Rule moves beyond this negative formulation. It is not simply about avoiding harm or hateful activity. By Hillel's formulation, we could avoid anything harmful simply by refraining from any contact at all with another. One could observe this part of the Golden Rule in splendid isolation.

An active formulation of the rule to love our neighbor is perhaps best articulated by a verse in the Torah: "You shall not stand idly by your neighbor's blood" (Leviticus 19:16). We must take positive action to rescue our fellow human when he or she is in danger. We must be prepared to meet another's needs when that person is in trouble. We must give a percentage of our income to help the poor and the needy.

In the previous chapter, I spoke of how deeds of loving-kindness become a way of imitating God. As God clothed the naked, so we clothe the naked; as God visited the sick, so we visit the sick; as God buried the dead, so we bury the dead; as God comforted the mourners, so we comfort the mourners (Sotah 14a).

One of the defining events of our modern time was the murder in New York of Kitty Genovese. As she screamed for help, dozens of neighbors turned their backs and took no action. Nobody was willing to take action to rescue her, or even to call the police. This incident provides an extreme example of our privatized, isolated, lonely society.

Community is about reaching out and helping others. It is not simply about avoiding harm; rather, it merits being proactive to help those in need. Ultimately, we build a better world in the midst of community, working together.

> A man went before God and said, "Lord, show me the difference between heaven and hell." God first took the man to see hell. A group of people sat in a banquet room, with piles of delicious food on the tables. Nobody was eating, and everybody looked strained and unhappy. The man looked more closely and saw that no one had an elbow that bent, so no one could bring a fork to his or her mouth. God said, "This is hell."
>
> God then brought the man to a group of people sitting in a banquet room, also filled with delicious food, with everyone rejoicing and looking satisfied. The man noticed that here also no one had an

elbow that bent. God said, "This is heaven."

The man said, "I don't understand. What is the difference?"

God answered, "In heaven, they feed each other."

Concentric Circles

Community is a series of concentric circles. It begins with one's self and one's own needs.

Hillel taught, "If I am not for myself, who will be for me?" Our first task is to take care of our own needs. When flight attendants on airplanes give instructions before a flight, they always say, "Put your own oxygen mask on first, then put the mask on your children." If we do not make sure we are safe and healthy first, we will be in no position to help our children or anyone else.

The next circle is our family. We have an obligation to our parents, our siblings, our children and our circle of relatives. At the dawn of time, Cain killed his brother Abel. When God asked Cain where his brother was, Cain answered with one of the great rhetorical questions in literature: "Am I my brother's keeper?"

(Genesis 4:9). The answer is yes, we are our brothers' keepers. We are obligated to care for our families.

The next circle of care is our community, our neighbors. We care for our neighbors and meet their needs. We work with others to perfect this world. Our mission is to be part of a team effort, joining in the greater community and moving beyond self and family.

There is one other concentric circle, the one that encompasses all of humanity. The Torah teaches, "Love the stranger, for you were strangers in the land of Egypt" (Leviticus 19:34). Loving one's family or community is natural; loving the stranger, the one who is different, the person of a different race, a different faith or a different ethnicity, is more difficult. As in so many other areas of faith, we must overcome our natural inclination to distrust others.

Perhaps the most famous statement in rabbinic literature is the passage in the Talmud in which the Egyptians were drowning in the sea, and the angels of God started to sing songs of praise. God reprimanded them, "My children are drowning, and you sing songs of praise!" (Sanhedrin 39b). Even the Egyptians, the enslavers of Israel, were God's children.

The journey to community is a journey of love. We move from loving ourselves to loving our family, then loving our neighbor and our community, and finally loving the stranger. It means moving beyond ourselves and our own selfish needs. It is a life of service to others.

Guideposts for Your Eighth Journey: From Self to Others

1. As the Hippocratic oath teaches, "First, do no harm." Avoid any action that hurts another human being. Avoid gossip, which is quite prevalent, yet difficult to observe. Gossip is any discussion that lowers the esteem of another human for the listener. Learn to speak of ideas rather than people. Scrutinize all your actions to ensure that you are not harming another.

2. Avoid harming any people as a whole. It is easy to hate groups that are "different." Avoid ethnic jokes, stereotypes, hateful speech, and any other action that denigrates another ethnic group, nationality, race, gender or religion. Learn to judge people as individuals rather than as part of a group.

3. The next step is to shift from avoiding negative

actions to taking positive ones. Do a good deed for another human being. Visit a shut-in. Volunteer for a food bank. Tutor in an elementary school. Visit a nursing home. Comfort someone bereaved. Treat a child in need to a concert, a sporting event or some other special outing.

4. Begin with your immediate neighbors. Learn their names. Invite them for coffee. Offer to watch their homes and collect their mail when they are out of town.

5. Greet strangers with a smile. Ask people how they are feeling. Offer assistance to someone you don't know; carry someone's groceries. Give up your seat on public transportation to someone elderly or infirm or pregnant. Seek opportunities to perform acts of loving-kindness.

6. Become a joiner. Join a synagogue or church and find opportunities to volunteer. Join a civic organization or run for the board of your condo or homeowners' association. Join a bowling league, a club, or a professional organization. Volunteer for your local PTA, scout troop, youth group or school. Community means going out to where people are.

7. Work to make this a better world. Find some small project that will help perfect this world as a kingdom of God. Find other people who share your passion and join them.

A Life of Service

The Indian poet Rabindranath Tagore wrote, "I slept and dreamt that life was joy. I awoke and saw that life was service. I acted, and behold, service was joy." Too often people end up depressed and bitter about their lot in life. My first advice always is to go out and volunteer in the community. In service to others, people quickly learn to find joy and meaning in their own lives.

In serving others, we imitate God. It is God Who reaches down in love to us, Who is there when we need help and support. When the ancient Israelites built the tabernacle they carried through the desert, a question arose: From where will God speak to the people? So the Israelites built a replica of two cherubim facing one another with their wings touching, and they placed it at the top of the tabernacle. Then God spoke from between the faces of the cherubim. Thus do we find God where two human beings face each other and meet each other's needs. As we help others, we come to realize that

God is our Helper.

9

Recovery

The Journey from Sin to Atonement

Sarah saw the son, whom Hagar the Egyptian had borne to Abraham, playing. She said to Abraham, "Cast out that slave woman and her son, for the son of that slave shall not share in the inheritance with my son Isaac."

Genesis 21:9–10

Rabbi Eliezer said, "Repent one day before your death." His disciples asked, "Does anyone know on what day they will die?" Answered Rabbi Eliezer, "All the more reason to repent today, in case you die tomorrow, and thus a person's whole life should be spent in repentance."

Shabbat 153a

A *classic Hasidic parable tells the story of a king who had a son he loved very much. As the son grew up, the king began to see he was heading down the wrong path. The son's behavior became more and more difficult, and the king realized that he could not keep him in the palace.*

The king sent his son to a far-off village to be raised in the home of peasants. There the king's officers and spies were able to keep an eye on the son. The king's son grew up in the village but always maintained a memory of the palace where he had been born.

One day the young man said, "I am the son of a king, and I must return to my father." He began the long and difficult journey. Soon messengers came to tell the king, "Your son is on his way home."

The king immediately broke into tears. He told his servants, "I know it is a difficult journey. Go load up my carriage right away. I will travel and meet my son halfway."

In their old age, Abraham and Sarah were blessed with their son Isaac. God's prediction had come true, although Abraham was one hundred years old and Sarah ninety. Their celebration of the birth of their long-awaited son was marred by a difficult situation. Sarah feared that Isaac's half-brother Ishmael, born to the Egyptian woman Hagar, would be a negative influence on their son.

Ishmael was thirteen years old at the time and already heading in the wrong direction with his life. Jewish tradition teaches that Abraham so loved having a son that he failed to discipline Ishmael. He allowed Ishmael to follow his appetites, and soon the boy was headed for a life of idolatry. Would he set a poor example for young Isaac?

Sarah insisted that Abraham send Hagar and Ishmael away from their home. Abraham was greatly distressed by this, but God said to him, "Do not be distressed over the boy or your slave. Whatever your wife tells you, listen to her voice" (Genesis 21:12). Abraham sent Hagar and Ishmael into the wilderness with just a small amount of bread and a jug of water.

The story that ensues provides one of the most poignant scenes in Genesis. The water was gone, and Hagar left Ishmael under a bush so she would not see him die. She cried to God, and God opened her eyes.

There she saw a well of water. God blessed her and told her that Ishmael would become the father of a great nation. Both Jewish and Muslim traditions teach that Ishmael is the father of the Arab nation.

Abraham felt guilty for his treatment of Hagar and Ishmael. First, he felt guilty about not properly disciplining and mentoring his oldest son. He also felt guilty about pushing him out of his home. Certainly, he had obeyed God's orders, but he had also failed at a father's fundamental job: protecting his child.

According to a wonderful rabbinic midrash, years later Abraham traveled to visit his son Ishmael. He was met by Ishmael's wife, who told Abraham that he was not welcome in their tent. Abraham left a message for Ishmael: "Change the peg of your tent." When Ishmael received the message, he divorced his wife and remarried (Pirke D'Rabbi Eliezer 30).

Shortly afterward, Abraham traveled a second time to visit Ishmael. This time Ishmael's wife welcomed Abraham, and father and son reconciled. Years later, Ishmael would attend the funeral of his father.

This story reveals to us that even Abraham went down the wrong path, and the Bible explicitly teaches, "There

is no man who does not sin" (1 Kings 8:46). The biblical patriarchs and matriarchs were neither saints nor
superhumans. They were mortals who made all the mistakes humans make. The Hebrew word for "sin," *chata*,
comes from an archery term meaning "to miss the target." We all sometimes miss the target.

Humans Can Change

The ninth great journey is the journey of recovery,
the journey back to the proper path. There are two great
truths in this journey. The first truth is that there exists
a proper path on which we are to travel in life. The second truth is that when we find ourselves on the wrong
path, we can change.

One of the most famous scenes in Lewis Carroll's *Alice's
Adventures in Wonderland* occurs when Alice meets the
Cheshire Cat, known for the mysterious smile that would
not disappear. Alice asked the Cat for directions:

*"Cheshire Puss," she began rather timidly. . . .
"Would you tell me, please, which way I ought to go
from here?"*

"That depends a great deal on where you want to go," said the Cat.

"I don't much care where," said Alice.

"Then it doesn't matter which way you go," said the Cat.

This simple scene says a lot. If we do not care where we are going on the journey of life, it does not much matter which path we take. Conversely, if we do care, we will try to find our way to the proper path.

In each of the previous chapters, we learned about the paths we ought to travel:

- On the path of self-control and delayed gratification, we suppress our immediate appetites for the greater good.
- On the path of family commitment and love, we fulfill our responsibilities to our parents, siblings, spouse and children.
- On the path of financial integrity, we provide for ourselves and our families, and we develop a prosperity mindset that makes us share our wealth with others.
- On the path of good health and fitness, we care for the bodies in which we live.

- On the path of healing, we cope with sadness and tragedy and pain, and we grow from the experience.
- On the path of connection to the spiritual dimension of life, we approach the universe with gratitude and a deep sense of wonder.
- On the path of community, we connect to our fellow humans, meet their needs and live in service to them.

Finally, on the path to immortality we discover the mission that God put us on this earth to fulfill. As the Cheshire Cat so aptly taught Alice, only if we know our destination can we find our way to the proper path.

We all go down the wrong path occasionally in each area of life. We all make mistakes, misjudge, allow our evil inclination to overpower our good inclination, and hurt ourselves and those we love. It is the nature of living that each of us sometimes misses the mark.

We also have the ability to change our behavior and get on the right path. The ability to change is part of what separates us from the animal kingdom. Animals have a single inclination and simply follow their nature. We humans have both a good and an evil inclination (*yetzer hatov* and *yetzer hara*), and God has given us the power to change.

The following classic story teaches the difference between humans and animals.

A scorpion asked a frog to allow him to climb on his back and take him across a river. The frog replied, "Do you think I am crazy? You will be on my back in the middle of the river. You will sting me, and I will die." The scorpion said, "If I sting you and you die, then I will fall into the river and die, too." The frog thought about it and finally let the scorpion climb on his back. When they were halfway across the water, the frog felt a sting. He turned and yelled at the scorpion, "You stung me! Now we both are going to die!" The scorpion replied, "What can I do? It is in my nature."

We often refer to the animal kingdom when we speak of the inability to change. We say, "A leopard cannot change its spots," and "You can't teach an old dog new tricks." In the previous story, it is a scorpion who tells a frog, "It is in my nature." Animals simply follow their God-given appetites.

One miracle of being human is that humans can change. We can put ourselves back on the right path.

We use the word "repentance" to refer to such a change. Perhaps the idea is better encompassed by the Hebrew word *teshuva*, which literally means "to return to the proper path." As Rabbi Eliezer taught, do *teshuva* in case you die tomorrow.

We always have the potential to change. In counseling people who find themselves on the wrong path, I have found a fixed series of steps to be most useful. I guide people through each of these steps, helping them find their way back to the proper path. In doing so, they can release the guilt that eats away at their souls. Based on the work of Maimonides and other Jewish philosophers, I call these steps "The Seven R's of Repentance."

The Seven R's of Repentance

Humans can get back on the right path after we have gone astray. It is a difficult process but certainly doable. How do we go about changing? Following is the series of steps we each must take as we strive to follow the correct path:

1. Recognition. The first step is to recognize that a

particular action is wrong. The statements "Everyone is doing it," "It is not a big deal" and "It is simply my nature" indicate that we do not even recognize our misbehavior. The Bible speaks of Pharaoh hardening his heart. After the first few examples, the language changes to "God hardened Pharaoh's heart." Pharaoh became so used to doing the wrong thing that he did not even recognize it as being wrong. Wrongdoing had become part of his very nature.

Despite our rationalizations, we humans can discern right from wrong. We have eaten of the Tree of Knowledge of Good and Evil. We have the ability to know the right thing, to recognize the correct path. Only with that recognition are we ready to change direction.

2. **Responsibility.** It is not enough to say that a particular action is wrong. We must accept responsibility to change, not make excuses.

An example of avoiding responsibility is found in the biblical story of Cain slaying his brother Abel. In a famous midrash about this story, Cain blames God for the crime. The midrash teaches that Cain is like the thief who steals from a warehouse and blames the night watchman: "I am a thief. I was simply doing my job. You are a watchman. Why were you not doing your job?!" So Cain blamed God for allowing him to slay his brother Abel: "If you had only accepted my sacrifice to begin with, I never would have done this deed" (Tanhuma Bereishit 9).

It is easy to find scapegoats for our wrong actions. We blame illness, racism, the way we were raised, our nature and everything but ourselves. With the completion of the human genome project, it is easy to blame our genes: "We were hardwired to act this way from the beginning." Shakespeare wrote in his play *Julius Caesar,* "The fault, dear Brutus, lies not in our stars but in ourselves." A modern update might teach that the fault lies not in our genes but in ourselves.

In San Francisco, defense attorneys used the "Twinkie defense" to try to exonerate the murderer of Mayor George Moscone and City Supervisor Harvey Milk. This particularly egregious example of scapegoating blamed junk food for murder. Blaming someone or something for our misbehavior is the easy way out. Taking personal responsibility is a necessary second step.

3. **Remorse.** When we do wrong, we ought to feel bad. We live in an age of therapy in which guilt is seen as unhealthy. Psychologists and other therapists exert much effort to remove guilt and help us feel comfortable with our actions. In truth, guilt has a purpose. Guilt causes pain that makes us change our ways. Guilt is a catalyst for making necessary changes in one's life.

   Having said that, I want to differentiate between guilt and shame. Guilt leads to the statement, "I *did* something bad." Shame leads to the statement, "I *am* something bad." Guilt can be healthy if it brings real change. Shame is never healthy. No matter what we do in life, we are still infinitely precious in the eyes of our Creator.

4. **Restitution.** Restitution is the notion that actions have consequences and that we must pay the price for bad behavior. This point is at the heart of the Seven R's.

   First of all, restitution means apologizing to those we have wronged. Jewish law requires that if our apology is not accepted the first time, we should seek forgiveness a second and a third time.

If we are not forgiven after three tries, we have done everything we can.

Restitution also means facing the consequences. We must pay for any monetary loss someone suffered as a result of our behavior. We also must suffer whatever punishments are appropriate. Restitution may even mean something harsh, such as having to resign a position or serve jail time. Sometimes when my children misbehave, they will apologize. They are surprised when I sometimes punish them anyway, and they'll say, "But we said we are sorry." I am trying to teach them that sorry may not be enough, that actions have consequences.

It is never easy to pay the price for bad behavior. Nonetheless, paying restitution is the beginning of reconciliation with ourselves and with God.

5. **Resolve.** Only after we have paid the price are we ready to take action to change our ways. This means making a decision to strive to return to the proper path. The Talmud teaches that if we sin and repent, sin and repent, without the resolve to change, even praying for forgiveness on Yom

Kippur does not help (Yoma 8:9). We must make a decision not to turn down the wrong path.

Resolve entails making a decision to become a new person. I recall counseling a man bitter over behavior he learned his wife had engaged in years before they were married. I told him clearly, "The woman you are referring to is not the woman you married. She has changed." Resolve is the decision to change who we are, to become someone new. It is often one of the hardest decisions we will ever make.

6. **Recovery.** I call this step "recovery" because it grows out of the recovery movement and the popular Twelve-Step programs. We must turn to a higher power, to God, to come onto the right path. The Talmud speaks of a person who goes into a shop to buy a smelly cleaning solution. The shopkeeper tells that person to help himself. Yet when someone comes in to buy a fragrant perfume, the shopkeeper comes over and tries to help. The passage continues, "Resh Lakish said, if a man comes to purify himself, he is helped from above" (Yoma 38b). The Hasidic story at the beginning of this chapter is

really a parable about recovery. When the son finally seeks to return to the father, the father travels to meet him halfway. So does God meet us halfway as we move back to the proper path.

The recovery movement also recognizes that change is a difficult process that we must struggle with daily. I have always been skeptical of those who brag of instant transformation, of being "born again" and immediately changing their ways. A midrash teaches that the evil inclination is at first like a spiderweb and later like a heavy rope (Genesis Rabbah 22:6). To untie oneself from a heavy rope, to overcome one's evil inclination, is a day-by-day struggle, with success achieved one day at a time. In that struggle we often feel as if we are floundering. If we turn to God, He will throw us a safety rope.

7. **Repentance.** In the day-to-day struggle to return to the proper path, we are finally ready to prove if we have succeeded. Have we become the new person we set out to be? Maimonides, the twelfth-century Jewish philosopher and physician, described true repentance as the ability to face the same

temptation again but to take a different path, the proper one (Hilchot Teshuvah 2:1).

When I teach this to children, I often use this example: Every day a child walks past a particular candy store and steals a candy bar. One day the child sees a security guard and decides to change her ways. This is not true repentance. On the other hand, if she recognizes her behavior as wrong, feels remorse, apologizes, pays the storekeeper for all the stolen candy bars and has the same opportunity to shoplift again but refuses because she has truly changed her ways, this is repentance. Repentance comes when we have passed the test and proven a change in behavior.

The Torah tells the story of Joseph and his brothers, how the brothers in a fit of jealousy threw Joseph in a pit and allowed him to be sold into slavery. Joseph rose to become the second most powerful man in Egypt, feeding the hungry during the years of famine. When his brothers arrived in Egypt asking for food, Joseph tested them. He arranged it so that they could abandon the other beloved brother Benjamin to slavery. When his brother Judah stepped forward to save Benjamin, prepared to give himself as a slave instead, Joseph knew that his brothers had experienced true *teshuvah*—true repentance.

Should We Forgive?

One of the seven steps of repentance is to seek forgiveness from those we have wronged. We cannot return to the right path until we find reconciliation with those we may have hurt while on the wrong path. According to Jewish tradition, we have to ask three times for forgiveness. If after three times, those we have wronged fail to forgive us, we have fulfilled our obligation.

From this we learn that we must forgive if someone who wronged us comes forward with a sincere apology. However, this raises the question of what to do if we have been wronged and there is no apology. Must we forgive others when they have failed to take the first step? Must the forgiver take the initiative?

Many of today's religious leaders teach a theology of

forgiveness, even when there has been no apology and no repentance for the wrongdoing. One of the most extreme examples appeared in the news after the high-school shooting a few years ago in Paducah, Kentucky. Several students gathered in prayer were killed. Almost immediately, signs appeared on the campus naming the killers and including the words "We Forgive You." Many of the parents of victims were deeply wounded by this rush to forgiveness, without any confession of wrong-doing or sign of remorse from the perpetrators.

In truth, there is no obligation to forgive when the wrongdoer has not sought an apology. Forgiveness is a reaction to a wrongdoer's heartfelt act of remorse toward the person wronged. As a rabbi, I am often asked, "Why can't you Jews forgive the Nazis for the Holocaust?" My answer is that it is not my job to forgive, that only the actual victims can do the forgiving. And they can only do that in the next world.

The initiative toward reconciliation must rest with the wrongdoer. Having said that, there is still a valuable lesson to learn from Jewish religious tradition. The Torah teaches that "You shall not commit vengeance in your heart" (Leviticus 19:18). On one hand, one does not need to rush to forgiveness. On the other hand, an on-going bitterness often damages us rather than the one deserving of our anger. It is like a hot coal we hold in our hand to throw at someone else, but find ourselves being burnt instead. As Dr. Laura Schlessinger once quoted from an anonymous author, "Anger is a poison we take with the hope that it will kill our enemy."

How do we find reconciliation when someone who hurt us has not sought forgiveness? I have counseled many people who grew up abused by their parents. Must they honor an abusive father and mother? I have told them that they do not need to destroy themselves in order to honor parents. However, they do need to begin the process of healing themselves.

One way to begin healing is to ask why the perpetrator committed the wrongdoing. Jewish tradition differentiates between those who commit wrongs because they are truly evil and those who commit wrongs because they cannot control their appetites. Perhaps when we see wrongdoing as a lack of self-control, there is room for more compassion toward the wrongdoer. Some people simply never learn to control their evil inclination. That does not make them right. It does make them human. Perhaps recognizing their humanity is the beginning of forgiveness.

Guideposts for Your Ninth Journey: From Sin to Atonement

Perhaps the best way to give practical advice about the road to recovery is to walk you through the Seven R's of Repentance for one area of misbehavior. Let us assume, for example, that you are a person who cannot control your anger. (This is an issue I deal with too often in my rabbinical counseling.) The same steps can be taken for other kinds of inappropriate behavior, from drug addiction to overeating to sexual promiscuity.

1. The first step is *recognizing* that there is a problem. I have spoken with abusive husbands who have told me, "That is my nature. I tend to get hot under the collar." Some consider anger to be normal and justified. "If I did not blow off some steam now and again, I would simply explode." Anger certainly has a role in fighting injustice. But out-of-control anger is extremely destructive to those closest to us. Until you say, "I have a problem," you can take no further steps.

2. The second step is taking *responsibility*. You cannot blame your genes, society, racism, sexism, poverty, your upbringing, your family or the unfairness of life. You cannot blame the victim. "I would not have beaten my wife if she did not provoke me." "My kids made me so angry I lashed out." "If I do not scream at my employees, they will not do their jobs." Rather than looking outward, it is time to look inward.

3. The third step is feeling *remorse*. Feeling guilty is painful, but it is a pain that tells us we are on the wrong path. Guilt is the energy that drives the engine of change. It is not helpful to wallow in guilt, but it is necessary to use it as a stimulus to take constructive action. Perhaps most important, do not let your guilt lead to shame. If you start saying, "I am worthless," you are on the wrong path. This is not the time to put yourself down but to build yourself up. It is time for you to say, "I can be better than this."

4. The fourth step is giving *restitution*. It means offering a sincere apology to everyone you wronged through your anger. There can be no excuses and

no scapegoating. Do not say, "If you hadn't _____, I would not have lost my temper." You must give a full and sincere apology: "I was wrong and I am truly sorry. Please forgive me." You must also pay the consequences, however serious—jail time, a fine, resignation from a job, a public confession.

5. The fifth step is *resolving* to change. It means becoming a new person. Look carefully at yourself as a person with an uncontrolled temper. Put the image in your mind of a person whose anger is under control. Visualize and perhaps write down how you would behave with that control. Imagine the new you. Visualizing is one of the primary methods used by motivational speakers to inspire change.

6. The sixth step is *recovery*. Perhaps it is time to connect with one of the many recovery groups in your community, all of which use the Twelve-Step methods of Alcoholics Anonymous. All build their approach upon turning to a higher power. Turn to God in prayer and meditation for help in changing. All of these groups teach that recovery is difficult and painful, and it must be tackled day by day.

When you feel yourself losing control of your anger, pray to God for self-control.

7. The seventh step is *repentance*. It means putting yourself to the test to see if you have truly changed. What will you do when you face the same provocation? Will you behave differently? Assess your reactions. If you have consistently managed to keep your temper under control despite being provoked, congratulations—you have changed.

8. Once you have seen how difficult it is to change, it is easier to become less judgmental of others. Everybody goes down the wrong path in some area of life. The great sage Hillel taught, "Do not judge others until you stand in their place" (Avot 2:5).

9. Try to forgive. You are not obligated to forgive people who have neither changed their ways nor asked for forgiveness. Nonetheless, the act of forgiving can be therapeutic for you. A more forgiving society will certainly become a more kind society.

From Justice to Mercy

Jews gather on the holiest day of their calendar each year to ask for forgiveness. They pray that God move from His Throne of Judgment and sit instead in a Seat of Mercy. It is a day of prayer, fasting and *teshuvah*, attempting to return to the proper path.

Underlying the liturgy of the day is the belief that God waits for us to find the right path. God is there to help us turn our lives around, to meet us halfway. Though God is a judge, God's main goal is not punitive. God's main goal is to help us return to the proper path. Mercy, rather than justice, is God's main attribute.

Still, most synagogues have the words "Know Before Whom You Stand" written on the synagogue ark that holds the Torah. We are being watched as we behave in this world. There is a proper path we ought to follow, and ultimately

God is our Judge.

10

Mortality

The Journey from Temporal to Eternal Life

Take your son, your only son, whom you love, Isaac, and go to the land of Moriah, and offer him there as a burnt offering on one of the heights which I will show you.

Genesis 22:2

[Rabbi Tarfon] used to say, "It is not your job to finish the task, nor are you free to avoid it altogether."

Avot 2:21

A fox saw some beautiful grapes in a vineyard behind a fence. There was a hole in the fence, but the fox was too fat to fit through it. For three days the fox fasted, and finally he was able to squeeze through.

The fox spent several days feasting on the delicious grapes. When he tried to leave, he was once again too fat to fit through the hole. Again he fasted for three days until he lost enough weight to squeeze through.

So it is with life. However we enter life, that is how we must leave it (Ecclesiastes Rabbah on Ecclesiates 5:14).

In the end, God tested Abraham with the ultimate test of faith. Was he prepared to sacrifice his beloved son Isaac? How strong was his devotion? God told Abraham, "Take your son, your only son, whom you love, Isaac, and offer him as a sacrifice." Abraham arose early in the morning, saddled up his ass, took his son and began the three-day journey to Mount Moriah.

The Torah emphasizes the closeness of father and son. Twice it uses the phrase "the two of them went together" (Genesis 22:6,8). Once on the mountain, Abraham tied down his son and prepared to offer him as a whole offering. An angel called to Abraham and said, "Do not touch your son. Do not lay a hand on him. For now I know that you did not withhold even the one whom you most loved" (Genesis 22:12). Abraham saw a ram with its horn caught in the bush and offered it up instead.

There are many difficulties in this story. First, how old was Isaac? A casual reading makes him appear to be a little boy, but the rabbinic midrash teaches that he was a man of thirty-seven (Genesis Rabbah 55:4). The rabbis made their calculation based on the fact that Sarah was ninety when she gave birth and she died at the age of one hundred twenty-seven. Perhaps she died when she heard of her son's near-sacrifice. If Isaac was an adult, did he participate willingly in his own near-sacrifice? Should we be willing to sacrifice ourselves for a worthy cause?

A second question arises. The Torah describes Abraham walking down the mountain alone. Where was Isaac? The midrash answers that he went off to a *yeshiva* (school where God's law is studied) (Genesis

Rabbah 56:11). If Isaac went his separate way, is it possible that there was an estrangement between father and son? The next time they appear together is at Abraham's funeral.

Some commentators suggest that perhaps Abraham failed the test. His job as a father was to protect his son, not to offer him as a sacrifice. By offering his son, Abraham was following the common ways of ancient pagans who practiced child sacrifice. Maybe the test was whether Abraham understood the ultimate value of human life.

Abraham returned to his tent to learn that his beloved wife Sarah had died. Much of the rest of the story of Abraham deals with the purchase of the Cave of Machpelah as a proper burial plot for Sarah. Eventually Abraham himself would be buried there, brought to his final resting place by his two sons, Isaac and Ishmael.

The final test found Abraham confronting the ultimate question we human beings must face: the question of life and death. He must confront the sacrifice of his son, the death of his wife and his own mortality. He must depart toward the tenth and final journey each of us must take, the journey from life to death, or as many religious traditions teach, the journey from temporal to eternal life.

Therefore Choose Life

How could any father choose to sacrifice his own son? This question has haunted religious commentators, biblical scholars and clergy throughout the ages. Whole books have been written about it. How can we hope to understand Abraham's motives? The difficulty is that the story is so foreign to our modern sensibilities. Abraham, who argued with God to save the wicked cities of Sodom and Gemorrah, did not argue to save his own son's life! Abraham, who prayed all his life to have a son with Sarah, almost killed him!

Why was Abraham so willing to obey God's command? Perhaps the answer is that during the time of Abraham people had a different mindset about life and death. Life was cheap, death was common and child sacrifice was the norm. The ancient Canaanites, like the Aztecs on the other side of the world, regularly practiced human sacrifice. To sacrifice a human being to appease a demanding god was simply a way of life in the ancient world.

The Torah delivers a very different message. Life is infinitely valuable. Life is not to be sacrificed. God is a God of life, God is the life-creating and life-sustaining force in the universe. The Book of Deuteronomy teaches, "I set before you life and death . . . therefore choose life" (Deuteronomy 30:19). To be a partner in the covenant with God, Abraham first had to learn this fundamental lesson.

From the Torah's point of view, life is of supreme value, though the Torah does allow taking a human life under certain very limited conditions: self-defense, war, capital punishment and martyrdom. Even in these cases, though, later rabbinic law puts extreme limits on each. We are taught that when given a choice, we humans are to choose life. Human sacrifice, and other activities that cheapen or shorten human life, will not be tolerated.

The fundamental message of the Torah, which Abraham had to learn, is the infinite worth of each and every human being. In a pagan world where life was cheap, someone had to teach the message that every

human life is a divine creation. The bodily existence of
the human soul in this material world then assumes
supreme importance. Abraham's task was to teach the
world the preciousness of human life.

Questions of Life and Death

If life is the ultimate value, some difficult questions
remain, perhaps the most difficult questions of all: Why
must we die? Why do we not live forever? Why would a
God of life place us on earth where our inevitable fate
is to die? The Torah teaches that God said, "Now that
the man has become like one of us, knowing good and
bad, what if he should stretch out his hand and take also
from the tree of life and eat, and live forever?" (Genesis
3:22). Why did God not allow us to eat of the tree of life
and live forever?

Sometimes, with tongue in cheek, I refer to my community as "God's Waiting Room." Many seniors come to
live their golden years among the sunny skies, clear
waters and multiple golf courses of South Florida. When
they die, their families turn to me for funeral services.

Officiating at a large number of funerals has forced me to consider my own feelings about life and death. So have my own recent personal losses: my brother, my mother and my father. I regularly consider what it means to be mortal. I have said to bereaved families, "Only the body dies. The soul lives on in some other dimension." I know these words give comfort. But what do they mean?

The Torah teaches that God formed us humans from the dust of the earth and then breathed into us a soul of life. Thus, there are two aspects to our existence: a material one and a spiritual one.

The dust of the earth represents the material. We are embodied creatures living in a world of material objects. As such, we are subject to the laws of physics and chemistry. These include the law of entropy. Like all physical objects, our bodies must break down and eventually die. This is an inevitable law of the universe.

However, our existence on this earth also has a spiritual dimension. We contain the breath of God. As God is eternal and outside of time, so are we: Part of us does not break down, does not become more disordered, does not die. In Hebrew we call what does not die the *neshama*, literally "the breath"; in English, we call it "the soul." Because they are part of a material world, our bodies may age and break down, may be subjected to hurricanes and tornadoes, illnesses and cancer cells, random genetic diseases and automobile accidents. Our souls exist beyond the material world, and therefore they never age. Illness can devastate our body but cannot touch our soul. As the Book of Ecclesiastes teaches, when we die "The dust returns to the earth from which it came, the soul returns to God who gave it" (Ecclesiastes 12:7).

Why would God put an eternal soul in a material body? This is the fundamental question of religion. Some would teach us that this embodied existence is inferior to the spiritual existence we had before we were born and will have after we die. Some would view the material world as something we must tolerate until we can finally escape to a better spiritual world.

The notion that the material world is somehow inferior has a long history in Western thought. It was the belief of the ancient Greek philosopher Plato, who taught in his parable of the cave that this world is a mere shadow of the true world of ideals. It was part of the Gnostic philosophy that separated the material from the spiritual. It is taught by many Eastern religious traditions. The inferiority of this material world has become a key part of many New Age teachings. The dream is to escape from this material world, that a better spiritual world awaits us. Such thoughts have given great comfort to many people, particularly those who have suffered in this embodied existence.

The lesson of the Torah is the opposite. The ideal existence is a bodily existence in this material world. In fact, the dream of Judaism is one of *mechaya hametim*, that the dead will be resurrected back into a material body. God wants our souls to live a material existence. Our soul may return to God when we die, but we dream that someday we will once again become embodied. I will never say at a funeral, "Now they are in a better world." After all, the Book of Psalms teaches, "The dead cannot praise God" (Psalms 115:17). The real action is in this world of the living.

Why is this world so important? To find an answer, we must go full circle and return to the first journey, identity, from childhood to adulthood: *Our soul has a mission to perform in this material world.* The soul is here to play a small part in perfecting the universe as a kingdom of God. Each soul adds his or her particular piece to this perfection of the world. We each have a task to perform that can only be performed in this world.

So God takes each eternal soul and gives it an embodied existence, places it in a material world where, due to the laws of physics, it must age, break down and eventually die. If God wanted our souls to do a task in this world, why did God not arrange for us to live forever? Why must we age?

Let me suggest one answer. Imagine telling your child, "Clean your room, but you have as much time as you want." The child will never clean the room. If we have forever, our tasks will never be completed. It is a different matter when you tell your child, "Clean your room by this weekend, or you cannot play outside with your friends." Given a time limit, the task is completed.

The same scenario takes place on a cosmic level. We are given a task and a limited time to complete it. Aging is the sign that our time is not forever. We are mortal, and our bodies wear out. We must use our aging to refocus ourselves on our tasks in this world. What do we want to accomplish while we still have our mortal existence?

Our bodies will not live forever, but our souls will. Our souls need our bodies to do their tasks in this universe. Somehow, piece by piece, each of us must do our part in being God's partner in creation, in perfecting this world as a kingdom of God. Our mortality is a reminder of our sacred trust.

The Circle and the Chain

What does it mean to be human? The Book of Psalms reflects the sense of futility and sadness we experience as we face our mortality. In one of his most pessimistic moments, King David wrote, "Man does not abide in honor. He is like the beasts that perish" (Psalms 49:13). The physical bodies of human and beast alike must die.

Abraham came to teach us that we are not mere animals. Even though we die, our lives have a cosmic purpose. When we speak of the mission of each and every soul in this material world, we are describing a particularly human trait. The notion of each human soul having an individual mission separates humans from the rest of the animal kingdom.

Perhaps the best way to demonstrate the difference between animals and humans is with two metaphors, the circle and the chain. Animals live in the world of the circle. The human quest is to break out of the circle, to see life as a chain.

Consider the beautiful Disney Studios movie *The Lion King*. The movie begins with Elton John singing the theme song, "The Circle of Life." A baby lion is born and held high for all the animals to see. The song tells of a great circle, with events repeated over and over with each new generation. At the end of the movie, a new generation of lions is born, and the same scene is repeated.

To the animal world, life is a circle. Each generation repeats what was done before. The life of a lion or a kangaroo or a parakeet is almost precisely the same as the life of these animals one generation ago. If we went back ten thousand generations and looked at the way a lion lives, it would be more or less the same as today. It was the power of this circle that Disney Studios caught so beautifully in the movie. Birth, weaning, adulthood, procreation, death—the circle continues unchanged from generation to generation.

A book in the Bible also speaks of life as an endless,

unchanging circle. The Book of Ecclesiastes, tradition-ally attributed to King Solomon and perhaps the most cynical book in the entire Bible, laments the vanity and meaninglessness of life.

> *Vanity of vanities, all is vanity. What real value is there for man in all the gains he makes beneath the sun? One generation goes, another comes, but the earth remains the same forever. . . . All streams flow into the sea, yet the sea is never full; to the place from which they flow the streams flow back again. . . . Only that shall happen which has happened, only that occur which has occurred. There is nothing new beneath the sun* (Ecclesiastes 1:2–9).

One senses Solomon's depression and futility. Is life but an endless circle, with nothing new to show for it? Are we forced to relive the fate of our parents and grandparents? If we are mere animals, forced to relive the same thing over and over, how can there be any ulti-mate purpose to life? The circle as a metaphor may work for animals, but not for human beings.

In his bestselling book *The Gifts of the Jews*, Thomas

Cahill wrote that the ancient Israelites, beginning with Abraham, gave the world a new metaphor:

> *All evidence points to there having been, in the earliest religious thought, a vision of the cosmos that was profoundly cyclical. . . . The Jews were the first people to break out of this circle, to find a new way of thinking and experiencing, a new way of understanding and feeling the world* (Cahill, 1998, p. 5).

The ancient pagan world, like the animal world, saw life as an endless repetitive circle. The gift of the Bible was the vision that we humans can rise above that circle, that we are more than mere animals. When God told Abraham to go forth from his home, God was telling him to break out of the circle and to find something new. Abraham introduced a brand-new vision of the purpose of living to humanity.

The Bible introduces a new metaphor, one with a beginning and an end. It is best represented by a chain, with each generation a new link. That is why the Bible is so concerned with who begat whom. Each generation builds and adds to the previous link. Previous generations contain a repository of wisdom and knowledge upon which a new generation can build. New generations stand on the shoulders of their parents and grandparents. Each new generation sees itself as closer to the perfect messianic age still to come. Humans experience a link between generations, an appreciation of the past and a vision of the future, which animals can never know.

This is the meaning of being human. To be part of a chain, part of some greater purpose, gives human life its spiritual quality. Now we can finally understand the beautiful thought articulated by the Christian theologian Reinhold Niebuhr and quoted in chapter 8:

> *Nothing that is worth doing can be achieved fully in our lifetime; therefore we are saved by hope.*

We each have a task to perform in this world. Rabbi Harold Kushner has written that death is not the tragedy. The tragedy is dying before we have had the opportunity to perform our task. To quote Kushner:

> *I am convinced that it is not the fear of death, of our lives ending, that haunts our sleep so much as the fear that our lives will not have mattered, that as far as the world is concerned, we might as well never have lived* (Kushner, 1986, p. 20).

That is why Rabbi Zusya, in the story at the beginning of chapter one, cried before his death, "Perhaps I was not Zusya."

We each have our own task in the chain of human existence. As Rabbi Tarfon used to say, "It is not our job to finish the task, nor are we free to avoid it altogether" (Avot 2:21). By completing our God-given task, we add our unique link to the chain of human existence. Unlike the parable of the fox at the beginning of this chapter, we do not leave the world the way we found it. We can go to our eternal life knowing that this world is a better place because we lived here.

Guideposts for Your Tenth Journey: From Temporal to Eternal Life

1. One of the most difficult tasks each of us must face is the reality that someday we will die. The more we plan our own death, the less a burden we become for those who survive us—our spouses, our children. It is vital to make plans now, particularly if you have reached your middle years.

   Who will have power of attorney to handle your legal affairs if you are incapacitated? Who will have the right to make medical decisions regarding your care? Have you made funeral arrangements? (It is always cheaper and more convenient to arrange these while alive.) Do you have life insurance to protect your family's finances if you are no longer here? Do you have a will to determine where your assets will go, including jewelry, furniture, automobiles and other personal effects? If you have a large estate, have you done the appropriate estate planning to minimize the tax burden? Have you made arrangements for your synagogue, church or other charitable institution to receive a bequest? It may be painful to deal with these questions, but it is far more painful for your loved ones to deal with them when you are incapacitated or gone.

2. Make an ethical will. It is an ancient Jewish tradition to pass to your heirs not simply your wealth, but also your values. Write down what is important to you and what you want your family to learn from you. What is your history? What are your values? How do you want your children and grandchildren to live?

3. Imagine your own funeral. Who would eulogize you? What would your rabbi or other clergy say

about you? What would your spouse or children say? What would your coworkers say? What would your neighbors and friends say? What would your epitaph say? If you are not happy with what you imagine being said about you, it is not too late to change your ways.

4. Review chapter 1 and consider your life mission again. What do you want to accomplish while still in this world? What legacy do you wish to leave? How do you want to be remembered?

5. Perhaps most important, learn to embrace life. Life is both extremely fragile and infinitely precious. Take time to enjoy the people you love. Spend priceless moments with the people most important to you—your parents, your siblings, your spouse, your children and your friends. Let go of anger and learn to forgive. Look for the positive and not the negative in life. Give people the benefit of the doubt. Learn to greet people with a smile and a friendly word.

6. As the Torah teaches, "Choose life."

Facing Our Mortality

Each of us must face our mortality. Each of us must walk through the valley of the shadow of death. It is the ultimate journey, the most difficult one each of us must face.

Some have sought comfort in the belief that this physical world does not really matter, that true spiritual bliss will be experienced in the world to come, that this world is simply to be tolerated until we are worthy of leaving for "a better world."

It is much more useful to see this material world as precisely the one where we have a holy task to perform. We are God's partners in the perfection of God's creation. God gave our eternal souls a material existence because we have a mission to perform in this world.

Ultimately, we are God's partners in bringing about the redemption of this world. We will add our own particular link to the chain of humanity, taking comfort in the fact that over the course of history

God is our Redeemer.

Epilogue

And Abraham breathed his last, dying at a good ripe age, old and contented, and he was gathered to his kin.

Genesis 25:8

Rava taught, at the time when a man goes for his final judgment they say to him, "Were you honest in your business dealings? Did you set aside a fixed time to study Torah? Have you practiced the mitzvah of 'Be Fruitful and Multiply'? Did you look forward toward redemption?"

Shabbat 31a

The rabbi stood at the harbor with his students watching two ships. One was leaving on a long journey; the other was coming into port after a long journey.

The rabbi said to his students, "We humans can learn something profound from those two ships. See that ship leaving the harbor. Everybody looks sad and apprehensive. The voyage will be long and dangerous, and no one knows if the ship will complete its journey successfully. See the other ship coming into the harbor. Everybody is joyous. It has successfully completed its journey and returned safely to the harbor."

The rabbi continued, "In real life it is the other way around. A baby is born and everyone celebrates. Yet no one knows if that baby's journey through life will be full and successful. A person dies and everybody mourns. Yet if that person has had a successful journey through life, we ought to feel great comfort and joy" (Adapted from Tanhuma Vayakhel).

The journey of life begins when God breathes the breath of life *(neshama)* into inert physical matter. A human being is formed. An eternal soul must now live an embodied existence in this material world. An ancient rabbinic legend tells that while the soul is still in its mother's womb, an angel teaches it everything it needs to know. A light illuminates the world from one end to the other and the soul knows the entire truth. Then when the time comes to be born into the world, the angel touches the baby on the upper lip, leaving an indentation. The angel blesses the baby and says, "Be good and not evil," and then causes him or her to forget everything learned *in utero* (Niddah 30b).

Perhaps the meaning of this ancient teaching is that in the beginning we know the proper path of life. Perhaps if we search into the deepest recesses of our soul, the memory of that path still resonates. Perhaps we can uncover the proper path for an eternal soul placed within the confines of a material body.

The journey of life is really ten separate journeys. Abraham, our father, has been our mentor throughout this book as we examined the practical wisdom that helps guide us on each journey. This wisdom teaches that our eternal souls can accomplish their divine tasks during our brief sojourns in this material world. Let us review these ten journeys of life.

The first journey is *identity*, the journey from childhood to adulthood. It is a journey about leaving home and separating from our parents. It means learning to honor the parents who raised us while establishing our separate identities. Perhaps most important, the first journey is about finding our unique mission in life. To begin, why did God send our souls here? What do we want to accomplish in our limited time upon this earth?

The second journey is *maturity*, the journey from self-indulgence to self-control. In this journey we rise above our animal nature and learn that life is not simply about satisfying our appetites. Success in life begins with self-control, self-discipline and delayed gratification. Success, and ultimately happiness, comes through hard work. Fulfilling our divine mission may involve hard work and sacrifice, but as the rabbis so aptly taught, "According to the pain is the reward."

The third journey is *family*, the journey from loneliness to love. God taught that "It is not good for man to be alone." The soul must seek a soul mate to help it accomplish its task. Part of the purpose of family is to raise and mentor a new generation to continue our work after us. But whether or not we are blessed with children, this journey is about finding a life partner. It is about learning to love by learning to see the value and serve the needs of another human being.

The fourth journey is *prosperity*, the journey from sustenance to abundance. Our souls must learn to live in a material world, providing for themselves and their loved ones. Being a provider is an act of love. While meeting its material needs, the soul needs to develop an abundance mindset. God gave us a world of plenty, where we can prosper materially. At the same time, prosperity grows when we share whatever we have with others.

The fifth journey is *anatomy*, the journey from frailty to health. The soul lives an embodied existence. The human body is a unique gift from God, functioning in an almost miraculous way. The soul must care for the body through proper nutrition, regular exercise, sufficient sleep and adequate medical care. Nonetheless, as a physical system, the body is subject to the law of entropy. Ultimately it will wear down—someday it will die. The soul knows that it needs this body to accomplish its mission in this world.

The sixth journey is *adversity*, the journey from pain to healing. As embodied beings, we are subject to the laws of nature. Whether from random injuries, cancer cells, diseases, genetic mutations, infertility, or other hurts such as divorce, bankruptcy, disappointment and the loss of our dreams, each of us must face adversity. We all know pain. We ought to know that there can be healing, and that our journey through adversity makes us the kind of people we are.

The seventh journey is *spirituality*, the journey from doubt to faith. We may be embodied beings, but we also carry within us the spark of the divine. A dimension of existence goes beyond the physical material world, a reality that cannot be measured in any laboratory. It is possible to connect to that spiritual dimension. When we make such a connection, we feel the wholeness of the universe within our very being. We realize that our missions may be in this physical world, but ultimately they have a spiritual purpose.

The eighth journey is *community*, the journey from self to others. We begin by looking beyond ourselves to our families, then to the greater community. Ultimately, we learn to love the stranger, for we were strangers in the land of Egypt. We do not live our lives in isolation, but within an interconnected web of relationships. We do for others as they do for us. We must love our neighbor as we love ourselves. Our mission is not performed in solitude but within the context of humanity.

The ninth journey is *recovery*, the journey from sin to atonement. Being human, it is inevitable that at some point in our lives we will travel down the wrong path. The longer we travel down that path, the harder it is to change. Yet change is possible. We can rebuild ourselves and move onto the correct path. Change is difficult, but part of what lifts us above the animal kingdom is that ability to renew ourselves.

The tenth and final journey is *mortality*, the journey from temporal to eternal life. The soul must do its work under a strict time limit. Inevitably, "The dust returns to the earth from where it comes and the soul returns to God who gave it." At some point we must leave this embodied existence and pass our work on to a new generation. In doing so, we find ourselves a link in the chain of generations. We build upon the work of our parents and grandparents, our teachers and mentors; our children and grandchildren, students, and disciples build upon our work. Each generation joins God in perfecting the world. All of humanity becomes God's partner in completing creation.

In the end, like the ship returning to the harbor, our soul completes its journey and returns to God. Its work in this material world is finished, and new souls must carry on the tasks. When God finished creating the world, He looked out and saw that the world was "very good." Very good, but not yet perfect. Our role as humanity is perfecting creation. As we go about our tasks in this world, we should remember that we are not alone. As we travel on our ten journeys through this life,

God is our Partner.

References
and Resources

Books

Bellah, Robert et al. *Habits of the Heart.* New York: Harper and Row, 1985.

Buber, Martin. *I and Thou.* Translated by Ronald Gregor Smith. New York: Charles Scribner's Sons, 1958.

Cahill, Thomas. *The Gifts of the Jews: How a Tribe of Desert Nomads Changed the Way Everyone Thinks and Feels.* New York: Nan A. Talese/Anchor Books, 1998.

Gibran, Kahlil. *The Prophet.* New York: Alfred A. Knopf, 1993 (first published in 1923).

Gold, Michael. *God, Love, Sex and Family: A Rabbi's Guide for Building Relationships That Last.* Northvale, N.J.: Jason Aronson, Inc., 1998.

Kushner, Harold. *When All You've Ever Wanted Isn't Enough.* New York: Summit Books, 1986.

Labovitz, Annette and Eugene. *A Touch of Heaven: Eternal Stories for Jewish Living.* Northvale, N.J.: Jason Aronson, Inc., 1990.

Muller, Wayne. *Sabbath: Restoring the Sacred Rhythm of Rest.* New York: Bantam Books, 1999.

Niebuhr, Reinhold. *The Irony of American History.* New York: Charles Scribner's Sons, 1952.

Prager, Dennis. *Happiness Is a Serious Problem.* New York: Regan Books, 1998.

Putnam, Robert. *Bowling Alone: The Collapse and Revival of the American Community.* New York: Simon & Schuster, 2000.

Audiotapes

Jarow, Rick. *Your Life's Work.* Boulder, Colo.: Sounds True, 1998.

About the Author

Rabbi Michael Gold assumed the pulpit of Temple Beth Torah—Tamarac Jewish Center in Tamarac, Florida, in 1990. Previously, he served as rabbi of Beth El Congregation in Pittsburgh, Pennsylvania, and Congregation Sons of Israel in Upper Nyack, New York.

A native of Los Angeles, Rabbi Gold received his B.A. in mathematics from the University of California in San Diego. He was ordained by the Jewish Theological Seminary in 1979.

Rabbi Gold's previous books are *And Hannah Wept: Infertility, Adoption and the Jewish Couple,* and *Does God Belong in the Bedroom?,* both published by

The Jewish Publication Society, and *God, Love, Sex and Family: A Rabbi's Guide for Building Relationships That Last*, published by Jason Aronson, Inc.

Rabbi Gold has lectured throughout the country and in Europe on sexual ethics, infertility and adoption, family relations, and finding a mission in life. His articles have appeared in *Moment, Judaism, Jewish Spectator, B'nai Brith International Jewish Monthly* and numerous other publications. He served as cochair of the Rabbinical Assembly committee on human sexuality. His weekly spiritual message goes to hundreds of readers throughout the world.

Rabbi Michael and Evelyn Gold are the parents of three children. He can be reached through his Web site at *www.rabbigold.com.*

From Simcha Press

Converting to Judaism is filled with amazing stories of re-creation—the extraordinary adventure of becoming a Jew at the turn of the 21st century.

Code #8202 • $9.95

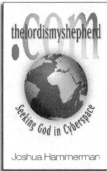

Joshua Hammerman

Code #8210 • $10.95

Experience the Net like you've never imagined —and find God! Travel through a world that transcends time and space, built upon the elements of creation.

Love Carried Me Home is a powerful, poignant examination of sixteen women's triumphant struggles to survive the Auschwitz Concentration Camp during the Holocaust.

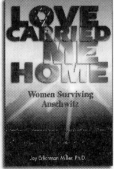

Esther holds within its pages an unusual love story that spans three decades and three continents.

Code #8245 • $11.95

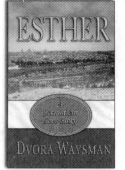

Code #8229 • $9.95

Available wherever books are sold.
To order direct: Phone 800.441.5569 • Online www.hci-online.com
Prices do not include shipping and handling. Your response code is BKS.

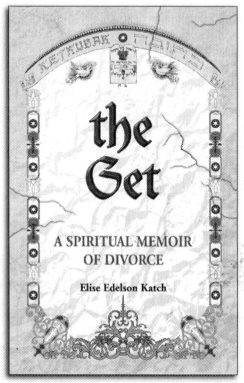